STORYTELLING MADE EASY

Persuade and Transform Your Audiences, Buyers and Clients—Simply, Quickly, and Profitably

MICHAEL HAUGE

INDIE BOOKS
INTERNATIONAL

ISBN-10: 1-941870-84-8
ISBN-13: 978-1-941870-84-6
Library of Congress Control Number: 2017935529

Cover photo by Jerry Metellus, jerrymetellus.com
Designed by Joni McPherson, mcphersongraphics.com

INDIE BOOKS INTERNATIONAL, LLC
2424 VISTA WAY, SUITE 316
OCEANSIDE, CA 92054

www.indiebooksintl.com

PRAISE FOR *STORYTELLING MADE EASY*

No one is better than Michael Hauge at finding what is most authentic in every moment of a story.

—Will Smith, star of *Men in Black*, *I Am Legend*, *Ali*, *The Pursuit of Happyness*, *Suicide Squad*, *Bright*

Michael Hauge has a masterful ability to help speakers, writers and marketers uncover the emotional potential of any story. He speaks and writes with the authority of a seasoned Hollywood screenwriting expert, and with his natural humor and likeability, helps us all apply those same powerful principles to our own speeches and storytelling.

—Patricia Fripp, past president, National Speakers Association, Hall of Fame keynote speaker, presentation skills expert

When I first met Michael and heard his six-step approach to story, I thought it was amazing. We incorporated his principles into our ClickFunnels software, which now has more than 30,000 active customers and creates millions of dollars a month in sales. Don't miss out on this terrific book!

—Russell Brunson, owner of DotComSecrets.com and ClickFunnels, Internet expert and super affiliate, author of *Expert Secrets* and *DotCom Secrets: The Underground Playbook for Growing Your Company Online*

I've seen firsthand with my mastermind group how Michael helps C-level executives formulate and transform their stories quickly and easily. Now you can as well with this simple but powerful book.

—Ron Karr, creator of the IMPACT! Formula, author of *Lead, Sell or Get Out of the Way: The Seven Traits of Great Sellers*

Storytelling Made Easy is brilliant! I've never met anyone that gets more excited about story than Michael Hauge. He understands, on a deep, visceral level, how to elicit that emotional impact your story must have. I can think of no better person to help you make magic happen.

—Andre Chaperon, Internet marketing legend. Writer. Author. Entrepreneur: tinylittlebusinesses.com

Keep this book within arm's reach at all times. Michael Hauge is a master at crafting stories that will increase your impact, your influence, your income, and your ability to promote your company, product, service or event.

—Mark LeBlanc, past president, National Speakers Association, author of *Never Be the Same* and *Growing Your Business*

Michael injects his Hollywood magic into your stories with just six simple steps. If you're looking to make your message more compelling and desirable, and to evoke a positive response from your prospects, then get your hands on this book!

—Matt Bacak, The Profit Coalition, 2010 Internet Marketer of the Year, author of *Secrets of the Internet Millionaire Mind, Marketing Sidekick*, and *Everyday Heroes*

An exceptional resource for any business owner
who is serious about moving onward to that next
level of success. Michael masterfully dissects the
Six Simple Steps necessary for any great story. His
real-world perspective comes from thirty plus years
of experience collaborating with some of the greatest
Hollywood actors, directors, studios and storytellers
of our time, along with top speakers and business
leaders from around the world.

**—Stephen Woessner, CEO of Predictive ROI, host of the
top-rated Onward Nation Podcast**

A must-have book that cracks the code for every
business owner, marketing person, and executive.
Hollywood storytelling expert Michael Hauge
provides a proven formula to quickly motivate
others with powerful stories.

**—Henry DeVries, speaker and consultant, founder of the New
Client Marketing Institute and the Marketing With a Book
Summit, author of *How to Close a Deal Like Warren Buffett*
and *Persuade with a Story!***

A brilliant book! Using what Michael has taught
me, I feel much more confident in my ability to
sit down and write a story that sells. It feels like
the stories write themselves...and writer's block
is practically a thing of the past. Knowing the
structure and key parts of great stories gives me
a framework that actually makes the end result
more creative and entertaining.

**—Jack Born, Software Entrepreneur: DeadlineFunnel.com,
JackBorn.com**

This book is dedicated, with deepest gratitude, to those of you who, through the power of story, have transformed my life:

Milton Arbogast, Charles Babbitt, Josiah Bartlet, Richard Blaine, Martin Brody, Hamilton Burger, Daniel Caffee, Elwood P. Dowd, Susan Evers, Allan Felix, Carl Fredricksen, Tom Hagen, Curt Henderson, Alex Hitchens, Gordon Lachance, Lars Lindstrom, Billy Mack, Sean Maguire, Kim McAfee, Annie Reed, Arch Stanton, William Thacker, Susan Walker, and David Webb.

Eternal thanks to you all.

TABLE OF CONTENTS

INTRODUCTION

Why Success Stories?

Are you a business executive? Salesperson? Consultant? Internet marketer?

Are you a public speaker, or do you give presentations in the corporate arena?

Do you write nonfiction books that guide people toward greater business or personal success, or greater happiness and fulfillment?

Do you use the media to establish yourself as an expert in your field, and to draw potential clients or customers?

Whatever your career or commercial endeavor, your job is always the same: you're a *problem solver*.

Every dollar (or peso or euro or yen or farthing or clam shell) ever spent, in every transaction ever made, was because someone had a problem they wanted solved. Something was broken and needed fixing, someone was sick and needed healing, someone was bored and needed entertaining, or someone didn't feel safe enough or wealthy enough or smart enough or sexy enough.

And the recipients of all hat money were the sellers of the products or services or experiences that buyers thought could solve their problems.

Why did those buyers want their problems (or their perceived problems) solved—or at least lessened?

Just one reason: they believed doing so would make them *feel* better.

They thought that if they—or their loved ones—had more money, or success, or possessions, or education, or fame, or approval, or excitement, or tranquility, or redemption, or laughter, then they would feel happier, or healthier, or safer, or more content or more fulfilled.

And they believed that the person or product or service they chose was the best one to provide that feeling.

In other words, any time someone pays you—or your company—they're making an emotional decision.

So, imagine if every time you gave a speech, or wrote a marketing e-mail, or published a book, or made a sales pitch, or tried to inspire an employee, you gave your audiences or readers or potential buyers the emotional experience of solving their problems?

What if you could give them an actual taste of the relief or the satisfaction or the happiness or the success that you're promising?

You can—by simply taking the steps that follow.

Stories That Sell

When added to speeches and marketing campaigns, stories increase e-mail response rates, client enrollments, product sales and revenue.

Why? Because well-told stories accomplish a multitude of benefits:

- They entertain

- They educate

- They inspire

- They hold the interest of listeners and readers

- They create a stronger connection between audiences and storytellers

- They deliver information in a simpler, more involving way than facts, figures, and diagrams

- And they move people to *action*

But they also achieve one more powerful goal: they give listeners and readers the emotional experience of success.

Almost anyone involved in sales or marketing or public speaking of any kind is already telling lots of success stories. But often these anecdotes and case studies are either overly brief, focusing only on the buyer's results ("Lily Rosebottom bought our new FatBeGone pill and lost fifty pounds!"), or they go on and on, meandering repetitively without clearly defined goals, conflicts, or outcomes for their characters.

Such stories can still entice buyers, but seldom will they sustain the interest of potential customers and clients, add real credibility to the product or service being offered, or overcome all the obstacles that stand between you and financial success.

A truly effective story must possess certain key elements, and must be presented in such a way that your potential buyer, client, or subscriber identifies with the hero of that story, and experiences the emotion of the story through that character.

When you tell a story about someone whose life was improved or transformed by your product, process or principles, your potential buyers must feel the way your hero felt when he succeeded.

With such a properly told success story, your target market has already experienced—on a subconscious level—the positive feelings that you are promising. And those feelings will move these potential customers closer to paying for your service or your product or your process.

In the pages that follow, this is the kind of story you will learn to create—simply, powerfully and profitably.

The Hollywood Lesson

My background is in Hollywood. I've written two books, created about a dozen audio and video products, and spoken to more than 80,000 people around the world about the process of writing and selling stories and screenplays.

And for more than thirty-five years I have worked with screenwriters, producers, studios, and movie stars, helping them create film and television scripts that will touch people deeply and powerfully.

When my clients incorporate the principles that follow into their scripts and films, they create a shift in the emotional state of audiences around the world, offering them the opportunity to connect with their own humanity, and transform their own lives.

So, what does this have to do with marketing stories?

Simply this: in 2016 Hollywood generated more than $11,000,000,000 in box office revenue. (That's 11 billion, if you lost count of all the zeroes.)

And that's just in the United States and Canada.

If you add worldwide box office, plus US revenue from all forms of video as well—DVD, online, and television—that number more than quadruples.

How does Hollywood do this?

By knowing how to tell stories, and by giving audiences the opportunity to feel something deeply. Because film and television makers understand that the primary objective of any storyteller must be to *elicit emotion.*

Movies are magic—they have the power to change people's thoughts and feelings, and to raise consciousness throughout the world.

In the pages that follow, I want to share with you a bottled version of this magic, so that you can change the hearts and minds of your prospects, and ultimately help them make buying decisions that can transform their lives.

The storytelling principles and methods Hollywood uses aren't limited to movies and TV. They are universal. They will elicit emotion and move audiences and readers to take action regardless of how they're packaged.

This means that when you follow the process I reveal in this book, you'll be using the same magic formula that Hollywood has been using so successfully for more than a century.

What to Expect From This Book

My goal is to remove the fear, frustration, and overwhelmed feeling that can accompany the thought of writing or telling stories—especially if you're not a professional storyteller.

Using the Six Step Success Story process will give you a powerful tool that you can use easily, repeatedly, and profitably. It will empower you to:

- Select the type of story best suited to your product or service

- Develop that story to skillfully target your prospective buyers, your potential clients, your audiences, or your associates

- Identify the most effective hero for each story you tell

- Apply the most effective overall structure to each story

- Employ the six steps of every successful success story

- Easily master a simple, entertaining, and persuasive writing style that is uniquely your own—even if you got Ds in English, and you don't think you can write a decent grocery list, let alone a compelling story

- Apply the principles of great storytelling within a variety of arenas: e-mails, speeches, instructional stories, videos, podcasts, and testimonials

- Apply the principles of wound, fear, identity, essence, and courage to move your readers and audiences toward more connected and fulfilling lives

That's a tall order, I know, but after witnessing the power of storytelling on readers, audiences, and writers for almost four decades, I truly believe all these rewards are within your grasp.

Storyphobia

I'm guessing that by now you're thinking:

"Of course, storytelling is essential to being successful. I've been hearing that since I started working. But I'm not a storyteller! I don't have a gift for it. I get confused or overwhelmed when I try to learn it, and terrified at the thought of doing it. What do you expect me to do?"

I know that the thought of anyone reading a story you wrote—or even worse, hearing you try to tell one on stage or in a meeting—can be terrifying.

But it doesn't have to be. The Six Step Success Story process isn't advanced calculus, and it definitely doesn't require high-level writing skills (which can actually diminish the power of your story). It only requires your willingness to give it a try.

Once you do, creating success stories will actually be fun. And you'll be able to transform the lives of a lot more people.

How to Use This Book

Here is how I recommend you make the best use of the principles and tools that follow:

1. Download your free Success Story Mind Map by going to www.StoryMastery.com/mindmap.

2. Read through chapter 1, just to get an overall sense of where we're headed.

3. Starting with chapter 2, select a single success story or case study about someone who has benefitted from the product or service or process you are marketing, or that you believe will change people's lives. (The chapter will give you a lot more guidance in how to do this.)

4. Develop this one story as you go through and learn the essential tools for writing about this person's (or this company's) journey to success. In other words, write the first draft of

this story as you progress through chapters 2 through 7.

5. Using the techniques in chapter 8, rewrite the story to sharpen its style, structure, and power.

6. When the story is as good as you can get it (which doesn't mean perfect—you're still in learning mode), ask some friends, colleagues, mentors, or satisfied clients to take a look and give you honest feedback.

7. While you're awaiting their responses, read the rest of this book.

8. Use the feedback you get to do a final polish of your story.

9. Send the story into the world—in an e-mail, a speech, a company presentation, or a blog. (This will probably be a scary step, so first read chapter 12: Your Own Hero's Journey.)

10. Begin the process again with your next story—this time an autobiographical story about a past success of your own.

11. From there on, just keep applying the principles to new success stories, and to the

other forms of storytelling that will grow your business to even greater levels of success and fulfillment.

12. As you continue increasing your expertise (and success!) at creating and employing stories, keep visiting www.StoryMastery.com to gain additional tools and insights, and to learn about opportunities to work with me directly.

That's it. Time to start your journey into powerful—and profitable—storytelling.

CHAPTER 1

The Six Steps

Every story ever told, ever written, or ever shown on a stage or a screen, is built on a foundation of three essential elements:

Character

Desire

Conflict

In every movie and TV episode, every novel and short story, every play, opera, epic poem, and fairy tale, a character (or characters) wants to achieve some compelling goal, and must overcome difficult obstacles to do so.

This character—the hero of the story—is our vehicle through which we experience the story. His or her desire propels the story to its resolution, and the conflict creates the emotion.

Whether it's Romeo wanting Juliet, Winnie the Pooh wanting some honey, a stranded astronaut wanting to survive on Mars, or a chemistry teacher wanting to provide for his family by selling crystal meth, when we read or see these stories, we subconsciously become these characters as they pursue their desires. And we feel for them because of the obstacles they must overcome.

Therein lies the power of stories: they give us emotional experiences outside the bounds of our everyday lives. We laugh, or cry, or get scared, or fall in love, or tap our hidden powers because we inhabit the stories we hear. *We* are the ones having those adventures, and facing those obstacles, just as those characters do.

And so it is with stories used for marketing, or persuading, or inspiring. They get readers and audiences not just to think, but also to feel.

Whether or not a prospective customer or client or crowd takes action—whether they hire you or buy your product or follow your advice—is ultimately an emotional decision. So, the more emotionally involving your stories, the more successful you will be.

The ways you accomplish this goal—the methods for making your stories powerful and persuasive—are basically the same for you as they are for successful novelists and screenwriters and filmmakers. Because your stories, like theirs, are built on those same elements of character, desire, and conflict. And your stories, like theirs, will always follow the same basic *structure*.

Plot Structure

Story structure—or plot structure—determines the sequence of events in any story.

Your goal as a storyteller is to maximize the positive emotional experience for your readers or audiences. By skillfully addressing the questions, "*What Happens?*" and "*When Does It Happen?*" you ensure that your potential buyers will connect with your hero, root for that character through the entire story, and celebrate his or her victory. And then they will want to replicate that hero's success in their own lives.

I've been teaching and coaching writers and filmmakers about structure since I began working in Hollywood. And while the basic formula for movie structure is fairly easy to explain, mastering all the variations and layers and principles involved takes a good amount of practice.

So, for our purposes, I've made it a lot simpler: success story structure consists of just six simple steps.

Six Step Success Stories™ are built on the six "stops" your hero must make on her journey to victory—the six story beats that will also ensure your own success as a storyteller.

When I use the term hero I simply mean the protagonist or main character of your story. This is the man or woman (or in some instances, the couple) whose desire will drive the story forward. It's the person we're rooting for.

I use the terms "customer," "client," "subject," and "case study" interchangeably, because every one of these refers to the main character or protagonist of the story you're telling. These are the people whose success was the result of the product or process or coaching that you're marketing.

Similarly, you'll see me use the words "potential buyer," "potential client," "reader," "listener," and "audience" to refer to the people reading your success story (if you're presenting it in a book, blog, or marketing e-mail) or hearing it (in your speech or webinar or recording or face-to-face meeting). Just substitute whichever of these terms applies to your own situation.

Because a hero can be either gender, I will sometimes refer to the hero as "he" and sometimes "she." That way you won't have to keep reading the cumbersome phrases "he or she" or "his or her." Trust me, you'll thank me for this.

The six simple steps will form the spine of every story you tell. And whether your goal is making a sale, landing a new client or inspiring an audience, these six steps are essential to achieving your desired outcome.

A Glimpse of the Six Steps

To give you an overview of where we're headed, what you will learn, and the process you will master, here are all six steps in sequence, with a very brief description of what you will accomplish with each one.

➤ STEP ONE: The Setup

You will begin your story by revealing the everyday life your hero was living before he heard about—or began using—your product or service. This "before picture" will create empathy for your hero, so your readers and audiences can experience his success on an emotional level.

➤ STEP TWO: The Crisis

Once you've painted a picture of your hero's former everyday life, you will reveal the single event that forced him to solve his problem—the moment where things got so desperate, or the prospect of change became so appealing, that he had to do something.

But before he could move forward, your hero had

to formulate a specific goal, and then figure out how he was going to solve his problem and achieve that outcome. So, you'll reveal how he researched, and hesitated, and asked a lot of questions, and considered other alternatives, until he finally chose you or your company or your product or your process to achieve it.

➤ STEP THREE: Pursuit

Here you present the actual steps your hero took to accomplish his goal. This will give your potential buyer a clear (and emotionally involving) picture of what using your product or service, or what following your advice, entails.

➤ STEP FOUR: Conflict

Along with your hero's forward progress, you must also reveal the external and internal obstacles he faced as he followed your program or used your product. It's the conflict in the story that elicits emotion in your audience. And by including the hurdles and setbacks that your hero encountered—and overcame—you will give your buyers the emotional experience of solving problems they are already anticipating (and worrying about).

➤ STEP FIVE: The Climax

This will be the peak moment of your story—the victory your hero was striving for, and that your readers and listeners have been rooting for: when your hero overcomes that final obstacle, crosses the finish line—and wins!

➤ STEP SIX: The Aftermath

This is simply the "after picture" of your hero's story—the new life he is living as a result of achieving his goal. It will show your readers and audiences the future that can be theirs if they only follow in your hero's footsteps.

That's it. These are the six simple steps of a great story.

Now let's explore each of these elements in detail as I guide you through the Six Step Success Story process.

CHAPTER 2

Selecting Your Hero

The hero of your story is simply the protagonist, the main character, and the person your readers want to see succeed.

By my definition, a hero is *not* someone who is heroic—at least not at the beginning of the story. It is someone who has the potential to *become* heroic. Finding the courage to move forward and achieve her goal (with the help of your product or guidance) is what will make her heroic.

A hero is a person—not a company or an organization or a group of any kind. If your case study involves work you did to rescue a business, or to increase its success, your hero will be the person who was most affected by the crisis, or who hired you, or to whom you were closest.

The Two Types of Success Story

In creating a case study/success story, you have two possible heroes:

1. Yourself. In an autobiographical story, you

are the hero. The story reveals how you transformed some aspect of your life by creating or employing the product, process, or principles you are now championing. (Or, on occasion, how you suffered some setback that taught you one of these principles.)

2. A Grateful Buyer. The heroes of these stories are former (or current) customers or clients who have improved or transformed their lives or their businesses by using the product or the system or the service that you're marketing.

Each choice has its own advantages, as you will see below. But the hero you choose determines the kind of success story you're going to tell.

➤ Autobiographical Stories

The more money you're asking potential buyers to spend, and the more you are promising them in return, the greater their desire to know who you are.

If I'm a potential client, and you're asking me to consult with you to increase my revenue, or to use a product you created to dramatically improve my health, or to sign up for a webinar that's going to cost me a thousand bucks, then I want to know your background, how you got to where you are, and if you're trustworthy.

The same principle applies if you represent a company you're asking me to work with closely, or if you're a boss wanting me to be more productive, or if you're a speaker hoping to inspire me. I still want answers to the same questions:

Who are you? Where did you come from? What do you stand for? And do you really understand my pain and my desires?

Telling me a story about yourself is one of the most powerful tools you have to create that kind of connection and trust.

Your autobiographical story could reveal how you achieved your own success using the process you're marketing. Or the human problem you witnessed or experienced that led you to develop, or make use of, your product. Or it might be an inspiring story of how you came to believe in, and practice, the principles that guide your life and your business.

Stories like these offer two huge benefits: they give potential buyers the emotional experience of participating in your success, and they create a greater level of connection with you because of your willingness to open up and share your previous pain and vulnerability.

But there are also some pitfalls that can diminish the effectiveness of autobiographical stories.

In my experience working with Internet marketers, their e-mails seem top-heavy with autobiographical stories, especially when their target market consists of other Internet marketers.

These stories often possess a quality of sameness. Marketing e-mails of the *"I hated my job/I became an Internet marketer/Now I'm a millionaire!"* variety are so common that they often seem manufactured and predictable.

The other danger in repeatedly making yourself the hero of your stories is that you can come off as egotistical, self-involved, or self-aggrandizing. It may seem to your readers that you're more interested in saying, *"Aren't I great,"* than you are in revealing, *"Here's how you can achieve greatness."*

Boasting isn't really the huge problem that many marketers or public speakers believe. Following some simple guidelines (which I'll reveal in chapter 10) will enable you to talk about yourself in a way that never comes across as bragging.

But always making yourself the hero of your stories limits both their appeal and their effectiveness.

➤ Case Studies

Stories about successful former clients and customers provide the most direct way of illustrating the power of your product or service.

By carefully selecting which of your grateful buyers or practitioners will be the heroes of these stories, you can ensure that your potential buyers will easily recognize their own problems within the story—and therefore hook into the solution you're offering.

Case studies also provide a multitude of possible heroes and stories to choose from. You can only go to the well of your own experience so many times. But opportunities to talk about other satisfied buyers are limitless.

And finally, case studies are pretty simple and straightforward. Somebody had a problem. They turned to you to fix it. Now they're happier, healthier, richer, more successful, or more fulfilled.

Autobiographical stories, on the other hand, involve a variety of personal situations and life transformations, forcing you to ponder which to choose, how open and personal to be, and whether you can truly be objective about your own life and the lives of those closest to you.

It's for this reason that the next several chapters focus on success stories about your clients, buyers, and followers. But as you will discover, you'll be an important character in most of these stories, as well.

Once you've mastered Six Step Success Story process, I'll reveal how all the same principles apply when creating an autobiographical success story. Then you'll be able to employ either type of story to elicit emotion—and generate revenue.

Finding Your Hero

The first step in identifying the hero of your success story is to comb through a list of past customers and choose a few that you know have benefitted greatly as a result of buying of your product or service.

I know this might be a huge list, but start with those who have told you about their successes and who have offered you testimonials. If you are a consultant, pick people or company executives you have worked with personally and guided to success.

Five such people should be plenty.

If you haven't heard even five success stories, just go to your list of buyers and ask for some. Send an e-mail saying you'd love to hear about the results they have achieved, and pick the best half dozen. (This is also a great way to get testimonials, as you probably already know.)

Now you want to pick the best of the group, based on these criteria:

- Prior to this person's (or company's) success, this potential hero was in a situation close to that of your potential customers or target audience.

Or at least this hero is someone to whom other buyers can easily relate, because they are similar in age, gender, occupation (or lack of), living situation, relationship status, health—anything that your buyer can recognize and identify with in his own life.

- This person's circumstances prior to using your product were negative in some specific way—he was very lonely, had a painful or debilitating medical condition, was stuck in a boring, dead end job (or had no job at all), had a successful business he wanted to expand to the next level, etc.

- The person you're considering is willing to talk to you in detail about where he was when he began his journey, and what he went through on the road to success. And he's given you permission to tell his story.

- When this potential hero purchased your product, he had a clear goal in mind—the more specific the better. Wanting to reach 20 percent body fat is more involving than simply "wanting to be in shape."

- The process of achieving success forced your

subject to overcome some major obstacles—both external and emotional.

- This person's success was directly due to what he purchased or learned from you. If he tells you that as soon as he bought a subscription to your newsletter he inherited $2 million, he's probably not your best candidate (though he might be a great prospect for buying your most expensive product).

- Having achieved the success you promised him, this person's new life matches your potential buyers' own dreams (e.g., financial freedom, independence, better health, travel, a beautiful environment, a fulfilling relationship, a thrilling social life, or a happy family).

The former client or buyer meeting the greatest number of these criteria should be your pick.

Doing Your Research

To determine how the list above applies to anyone you're considering, you need to interview your best candidates. These interviews will also provide you with the material for writing the success story once you've selected your hero.

Below are some sample questions you can use

as models for your own interviews. As you will see, the questions correspond to the six steps of a well-told story. Each is designed to provide you with more of the information you need to structure your story and to make it as vivid, emotionally involving, and persuasive as possible.

You'll just have to rephrase the questions so they're appropriate for the product or coaching that you're marketing.

I know the list seems long, but you're not going to ask your possible hero all of these questions—if you do, it will take him longer to answer them than it did to transform his life.

Instead, regard these interviews simply as conversations designed to get your potential hero talking about his experiences and feelings as he pursued his goal. Your primary job is to listen to what he says, record it, and use his revelations to guide you toward your next questions.

➤ Case Study Questions

Let's say you are marketing a financial program that has successfully empowered people to overcome massive credit card debt. You are interviewing someone who used the program successfully, and is now debt free.

Here are the kinds of questions you'll want to ask.

➤ The Setup

- *How did you acquire the debt you were in?*

- *How much did you owe?*

- *How did your financial situation affect your— and your family's—life back then?*

➤ The Crisis

- *What single event moved you to finally take action?*

- *What was your specific goal—how would you know you had finally solved the problem of your credit card debt?*

- *What, if anything, did you do to overcome your debt prior to starting our program? And why didn't those other approaches work?*

- *What made you decide to give our approach a try?*

➤ Pursuit

- *How did it feel the day you took that first step and began the program? Were you excited? Skeptical? Reluctant? Afraid?*

- *What elements of the program did you find most effective or beneficial for you?*

- *What surprised you about this process? Was*

anything about following our program different than what you expected?

> **Conflict**

- *What were the hardest things about starting, and sticking to, the program?*

- *Did anyone try to discourage you from continuing, or unintentionally make the process harder?*

- *How did you overcome those tough times—how were you able to push through the obstacles and setbacks?*

> **The Climax**

- *How did you finally know you had succeeded— that you had achieved what you set out to?*

- *What was that exact moment like for you?*

> **The Aftermath**

- *What is your life—and the lives of those around you—like now, compared to what it was before you began our program?*

- *What would you suggest to anyone else dealing with overwhelming debt?*

As you can see, these questions can easily be modified to use with someone who was desperate for a better job, or who was facing a medical challenge, or who wanted a more fulfilling love life, or who had always dreamed of being an entrepreneur, or an author, or a public speaker.

Appendix II offers a longer list of questions, including spaces for answers and notes. This list can be modified for any potential case study.

You can also download the list by going to www. StoryMastery.com/casestudyquestions.

Interviewing Loved Ones

Including your former customer's spouse or partner or parent in one of these conversations, or speaking to that person separately, will provide you with lots of valuable information and insight into what your hero went through.

A significant other can fill in a lot of blanks and give a different perspective on her loved one's problem. You will learn about all the challenges your hero's spouse faced before her loved one began his journey to success, and you'll get her own feelings about what that process was like. And knowing how the spouse's life has now changed for the better will lead to an even more powerful and persuasive success story.

You might even consider creating a separate success story in which your customer's *spouse* is the hero. Reveal her life as she struggled to help her husband, and the obstacles she had to overcome in supporting him, all the while dealing with her own fears and feelings. Then paint a picture of the new life *she* is leading after helping her loved one cross the finish line.

Think how powerful such a success story will be in influencing potential buyers who are desperate to get their own loved ones to take action, and to help them escape their feelings of despair and defeat.

Corporate Questions

So, what if, instead of marketing a product, you're a business coach or a financial consultant who wants to use success stories to attract corporate clients?

In these cases look for a company with a problem you helped solve. Then pick the person at that company with whom you worked most closely, someone who observed—and appreciated—the work you did, and who personally benefitted greatly from your guidance. This individual will be the hero of your story.

Though the specifics of this success story might differ greatly from our debt-ridden hero above, the thrust of the questions will be identical to those in the previous list. Just guide your interviewee through the six steps and ask what those experiences were like.

In Appendix III I've provided a complete list of questions you can choose from as you interview previous clients or customers from the corporate arena. You can also download the list by going to www.StoryMastery.com/corporatequestions.

As you will see, while the specific questions will differ, the overall approach to researching your potential heroes is identical.

And notice that these questions go beyond the company's financial figures and bottom line; they repeatedly focus on the emotional components of the journey as well. While some executives might not want to acknowledge it, these can be as persuasive to potential corporate clients as the dollars and cents outcomes.

Questionnaires

As a preliminary step to one-on-one interviews, you may want to poll satisfied customers about their experiences with your product so you can pick the best potential success stories based on their responses. And sometimes a one-on-one conversation simply isn't possible with a prospective case study, so written responses are your only alternative.

In these cases, you can't say, "I'd like you to answer these twenty-seven questions in writing." People have neither the time nor the desire for such an overwhelming undertaking, especially when you're asking it as a favor.

Instead, ask for written or recorded answers to just three simple questions:

1. *What were the circumstances that made you decide to work with me or use our product or service?*

2. *What was the process itself like, in terms of both successes and setbacks, from the time you began until you achieved your goal?*

3. *How has your life/business changed as a result?*

As you see, I've simply consolidated the six steps into three broader questions that will provide a basis for narrowing your hero search. Once you've done that, you can add any remaining details with just a few additional questions, or a conversation.

CHAPTER 3

Step One–The Setup

At last!

After identifying the hero of your success story, researching that satisfied customer or client, and organizing the elements of that person's or company's story into the appropriate steps, you finally get to start writing.

My mentor, Art Arthur, who was a successful movie and TV writer for more than fifty years, lived by this motto: *Don't get it right—get it written.*

The goal of your first draft is not to achieve perfection. It's to get something onto the page so you can begin building your story.

Start by simply listing everything you've learned about your hero's experience in chronological order. Break it into six parts corresponding to the six steps. Then, following the principles that follow, put it into paragraph form.

Once you do, your first draft will be finished!

I promise you'll think it's awful. It probably *will* be awful. But at least it will be *done*. Then all you'll have to do is edit it to make it better. Trust me, rewriting is a lot more fun than facing a blank page.

In chapters 7, 8, and 9 we'll address style and rewriting in much greater detail. Until then, stop worrying about what a bad writer you are (you're not) and do what every good writer does: get something written.

So let's dive in, starting at the beginning with Step 1: The Setup.

The Before Picture

When the hero of your success story first purchased or used your product, service, or program, she began a journey that would ultimately empower her to achieve her goal.

But for her story to be emotionally involving and persuasive, you must first show this hero's before picture—her life prior to beginning that pursuit. This will provide your readers with a basis for comparison to the life she'll be living once she succeeds.

What did your hero do on a day-to-day basis before she encountered you or your product? In what ways was she unhappy, unsatisfied, or unfulfilled? And what effect did this situation have on her health, her family, her business, her psyche, or her hopes for the future?

When we first meet her, your hero should be stuck in a state of inertia—struggling with a negative situation she doesn't know how to overcome, or tolerating a static existence because she's afraid of change, or because she simply doesn't believe her life or her business will ever be any better.

This kind of introduction provides immediate conflict for your story, as your hero struggles with whatever obstacles stand between her and the better life she longs for. And conflict, as you may be tired of hearing me say, elicits emotion—the primary objective of any well-told story.

The setup doesn't necessarily need to take us all the way back to the beginning of your hero's problem.

Let's say you're promoting a new product for Internet marketers. You might introduce your hero when she was already earning money in direct sales— but not achieving the level of success she dreamt of. She's not miserable; she just isn't where she wants to be in life.

Sometimes your setup will reveal that everything was going just fine for your hero. But this simply means that she was unaware of the major crisis to come.

Just be certain your setup reveals the negative qualities of your hero's existence that your product eventually alleviated. If your product promises greater wealth and independence, show how poor, desperate, trapped, or depressed your hero was before your product transformed her finances. Immediately illustrating the conflict your hero faced accomplishes one other essential objective for your story: it creates empathy.

Empathy

Stories are a participatory experience. Audiences and readers don't simply want to watch, hear about, or read about characters who laugh, or cry, or fall in love, or get scared, or celebrate their victories—they want to have those experiences themselves.

We become the heroes of the stories we love, as they face insurmountable obstacles in pursuit of impossible goals. We want to experience emotion through these characters.

As a storyteller, you must create an unbreakable bond between your hero and your potential buyers. They must identify with your hero so strongly that subconsciously they believe they are that character.

This is what is meant by empathy.

Here are the four most powerful methods for establishing empathy. As soon as you introduce your hero, start applying as many of these principles as you can:

1. Create Sympathy for Your Hero

We empathize with people we feel sorry for. By showing how your hero is, or has been, the victim of some undeserved misfortune, you increase our emotional investment in his success.

Perhaps your hero suffers from a debilitating medical condition. Or maybe he is alone and lonely, longing for a fulfilling relationship. He might be going through a painful divorce or bankruptcy, or maybe he's simply stuck in a dead-end job.

Any of these events or situations will ensure that buyers and audiences identify with this character.

2. Put Your Hero in Jeopardy

We identify with people we worry about. A hero who is in danger of losing anything of vital importance to him becomes far more empathetic.

He might be about to go bankrupt, or lose his job or his home. His business may be circling the drain because he can't compete with newer, cheaper, better-funded competitors. He might be battling a life-threatening illness, or he might simply worry that he won't score high enough to win his bowling-league championship. These are all forms of jeopardy that will increase your reader's empathy for the character.

3. Make Your Hero Likeable

Readers root for characters they care about. They want to identify with people who are kind, loving, generous, and good-hearted.

If the setup of your story introduces a hero who is trying to create the best possible life for his children, or who is donating time or money to a worthy cause, or whose job is to serve victims of poverty or disease or natural disasters, the empathy for your hero is strengthened. It's even stronger if you show how your hero is well liked or admired by others in his life.

4. Show That Your Hero is Highly Skilled

We are all drawn to people who exhibit extraordinary skill. Subconsciously, we want to become characters that possess physical or intellectual or interpersonal abilities that we mere mortals could never attain. Movies and myths give us superheroes. Success stories give us heroes who can get the job done.

In success stories, business leaders, financial magicians, high achievers, and accomplished experts attract readers and audiences the way superheroes, super cops, superspies, and super athletes do in the movies.

Highly skilled heroes draw us into a story. But once that emotional connection is established, they must still suffer crises and setbacks that will be overcome using your product or your guidance.

Perhaps you are a consultant whose former client had already found great success in his chosen arena. Then you helped him reach some new pinnacle of achievement. Readers and audiences will empathize with him because of his skill and success, while still rooting for him to achieve this new goal—with your guidance.

Notice that all four of these methods for creating empathy are built on conflict: *sympathy* for your hero's conflict in the past or the present, *jeopardy* from perceived obstacles looming in the future, *likeability* growing out of the ways your hero supports others facing their own hardships, and *skill* your hero has shown in overcoming past obstacles.

Once you've written the essential elements of your hero's life before he took action—the negative situation and the inertia and the sources of empathy—it's time to move your hero to Step 2, where he will experience his moment of crisis.

CHAPTER 4

Step Two–The Crisis

In the setup of your success story, your hero was stuck in a state of inertia. He may have exhibited a lot of activity and effort, but he wasn't really moving forward toward whatever outcome he longed for.

Now it's time to get him unstuck and on the path to transformation.

The Wakeup Call

No matter where your hero began, there was always that one event that turned him in a new direction and eventually led him toward you or your product. Describing that turning point will be far more emotionally involving than jumping directly from, "My customer was miserable," to "My customer started using my method."

It's possible your hero wasn't in—or wasn't conscious of—a negative situation when the crisis occurred. Maybe he was coasting along and things seemed to be going fine: good business, good health, a good relationship, and contentment.

Then everything went to shit. An order arrived for an impossible contract that his company had to fulfill in order to stay in business. An employee was caught stealing money, and the company faced bankruptcy. A spouse unexpectedly left. A job was a victim of downsizing.

In these stories, the crisis itself provides much of the undeserved misfortune or jeopardy that will ensure empathy with your hero.

But in most success stories, the hero had been tolerating some negative situation for a long time, and the crisis was simply the opportunity, or the new piece of information, that spurred the hero to action.

Maybe your hero's wakeup call was the night she went on her fifth horrid date in a row, and simply had to find a new way to meet eligible men. Perhaps this was the moment your hero, whose company had been on the rocks for months or years, first heard about your product, or your program, or your consulting service. Or perhaps it was the day she first learned about other consultants she thought could solve her problems (but ultimately didn't solve them, forcing her to hire you).

If you're a digital marketer promoting your process to other digital marketers, this could be when your hero first learned about the potential for direct sales. Or if your setup portrays a hero who was already selling things online, but not getting the results he hoped for, this could be the day when someone recommended your particular method for multiplying his revenue.

Whatever the starting gun for your hero's journey, don't skip this step. Your audience needs to be there at the beginning, when your hero finally takes the step you want her to take.

And be specific. Don't simply write, "He couldn't take it anymore," or "He decided things had to change." Describe that exact moment when the roof caved in, or the straw broke the camel's back, or whatever other cliché finally occurred.

The Goal

When the crisis reached a boiling point and your hero began taking action against the pain he was feeling, what was the life, or the accomplishment, or the transformation he wanted instead? What, exactly, was the goal he was desperate to achieve?

Your hero isn't yet ready to begin using your method or product to achieve this desire. But your readers and audiences want to know where this journey is headed—and what exactly they're rooting for.

The more specific and visible you make this goal, the stronger your story will be.

Be as clear as possible about the finish line your client or buyer wanted to cross (even if, in real life, your hero's goal was only vaguely formulated). Of course your hero wanted to be wealthy or healthy or happy or independent. But those goals aren't *vivid*. You must create a picture of what success will look like for your hero—a clear image of exactly what that accomplishment will be.

A desire to "get rid of arthritis" creates a very fuzzy image. But we can clearly envision a father able to walk his daughter down the aisle without crippling pain.

"Getting rich," "getting in shape," and "being happy" don't give your audiences much to anticipate or root for. But a bank account statement with a balance of $100,000, crossing the finish line of an Ironman triathlon, sitting on a beach at a resort in Fiji—these are far more emotionally involving outcomes.

If you're a consultant, oftentimes you will confront your client with this very issue. They come to you with a vague notion of saving their company, and you ask them, "What exactly would that look like to you? How will you know when your company is 'saved'?

What measurable results are you looking for?"

The more tangible the results your client wants to achieve, the easier it will be to guide him toward that finish line. And so it is with the hero's goal in a success story.

Uncertainty

The crisis forced your hero into a new situation. His world was turned upside down, and he was thrust into unfamiliar territory, so he had to navigate this new terrain as he formulated a plan for achieving his goal.

Every Hollywood movie includes such a sequence. In *Avatar*, hero Scully arrives on Pandora and now must learn about the environment, the hostilities, his avatar, and the job he's been given. In *The King's Speech*, Bertie learns about an unconventional speech therapist, and now must meet Lionel Logue and decide if he wants to work with him.

In your success story, no matter how desperate your hero is, he won't immediately jump into action. He'll begin by asking questions:

How should I react to this crisis? What are my options? What are their costs, in money, and in time, and in physical and emotional stress? What will be expected of me? How much risk is involved? How do I know which one will succeed? And what will happen if I fail?

Notice that all these questions create another kind of conflict: uncertainty. When your buyer or client first encountered your product or your service, it may have sounded great, but I promise you he was skeptical. He had to be persuaded that it was worth whatever risk was involved.

Ineffective success stories mistakenly eliminate this element. The heroes of these stories learn about a seller's product or service and immediately plunk their money down and dive in.

Including this step lets you verbalize all the questions your prospective buyers are asking themselves—and then gives you the opportunity to answer them. Addressing the concerns your hero had in this way, and revealing whatever answers he arrived at, will alleviate a lot of the uncertainty and resistance your prospect is already feeling.

Using your story to illustrate the positive qualities of your product will sway your readers more than if you simply present them with facts, statistics, and arguments. Including this part of the journey gives your buyers (who identify with your hero) the emotional experience of making the right choice and saying yes to your offer.

When you interview your case study subject, he may reveal that before choosing yours, he purchased other methods or products, hoping they would solve his problem.

This is great news!

Including these false starts in your hero's story gives you a golden opportunity to reveal (through your hero's experiences and conclusions) what happened with those other products, and what makes them inferior to yours.

The failures or setbacks your hero experienced using your competitors' products—products that make many of the same promises that yours does— will be far more effective at luring potential buyers than if you simply claim, "Mine is better than theirs."

Commitment

At the end of this period of uncertainty and deliberation, describe that moment when your hero finally paid for, and began, your program. Some final fact, some encouragement from a loved one, or some gut feeling told her that this was the best way to face her crisis, solve her problem, and achieve success.

Find out from your hero exactly what was involved, and what it felt like, to make that commitment.

And as you tell her story, let your readers hear her

exact declaration regarding what she wanted. "That's when I told my husband, 'This is it. I'm going to begin this program, and in ninety days I'm going to launch my new website!'"

Notice that in this example I included a time limit for the hero to achieve her goal. Adding a "ticking clock" like this one further increases the conflict for your hero. And conflict elicits…well, you know.

I'll reveal more about deadlines and ticking clocks in chapter 9. But right now we have to propel your hero toward the finish line with steps three and four.

CHAPTER 5

Steps Three and Four— Pursuit and Conflict

As soon as the hero of your story commits to using your product, method, or coaching, begin taking your readers through the specific steps he took—and the obstacles he faced.

Again, you want to give your potential customer the emotional experience of working with you or your company or your product—and succeeding! Simply saying, "Once he hired me, his problems were solved and his life changed forever," won't do that.

Only by taking the journey *with* your hero will your readers or audience understand what's involved, and realize the specific benefits of what you're offering.

Taking Action

What was the very first thing your subject did once he made that commitment to your product? Download a program? Receive the product in the mail? Meet with you for an initial evaluation or consultation session?

Whatever it was, describe it. Create a picture of his actions.

What about his feelings? Was he excited? Nervous? Skeptical? Afraid? Describe those emotions as well.

Continue in this way through step three, detailing some of the specific actions your hero took as he pursued his goal. And let us *experience* what he did. Let us hear the sounds and feel the sensations that were part of the pursuit.

Your goal as a storyteller is to create a movie in the mind of your audience. Let them see your hero— and imagine themselves—as he moves closer and closer to victory through step three.

Incorporating these parts of the actual process not only propels your story forward, it gives your audience a much clearer picture of what working with you or using your product will be like. Instead of just telling them how simple or instructive or productive or motivating your process is, you're showing them what's involved.

Including every little detail or element of your hero's pursuit isn't necessary—or advisable. Pick just two or three key tasks your hero performed to achieve the desired outcome, focusing on those steps that make your product unique, and that make experiencing it sound fun and fulfilling.

Obstacles

Along with the steps forward your hero took, include some of the obstacles and setbacks he encountered as well.

For step four, reveal the conflict your hero faced: When was the process difficult? When did he get discouraged? Were there times when the outside world got in his way? Did friends or loved ones criticize him, or express sympathy and concern that he was working too hard or wasting his money? Was he ever tempted to postpone the process, or quit altogether?

And most important, *how did he overcome those obstacles?*

You might be reluctant to reveal such conflict in your story, for fear the thought of difficulties and setbacks will scare prospective buyers away. But I suggest you include them for two reasons:

1. Your goal is to elicit emotion, and (say it with me…) *emotion grows out of conflict.* The moments of struggle a hero faces are the most involving of any story.

2. Your prospective buyers are already concerned about offers and opportunities that sound too good to be true—because they've all flushed their money away on such products in the past.

If you openly declare that the process you're marketing isn't a piece of cake—that frustrations and setbacks will occasionally occur—you can then show your hero overcoming these obstacles to make even greater progress.

Now you've convinced your buyers that your product isn't some pie-in-the-sky fantasy, *and* you've given them the emotional experience of even greater success.

I don't know anyone who believes those magazine cover headlines promising six-pack abs in just five minutes a day while eating Karmelkorn. Making your process sound like a walk in the park will create more skepticism than persuasion.

If you're using this story to market yourself—as a coach or consultant or expert—including your hero's conflict allows you to reveal how, in the face of his fear and frustration and misgivings, you helped him overcome whatever was holding him back.

Continue describing step three and step four—the ups and downs of your hero's *pursuit* and *conflict*—in this way until he is finally on the verge of success, ready to cross that magical finish line…the *climax*.

CHAPTER 6

Steps Five and Six–The Climax and The Aftermath

No Hollywood movie has ever succeeded in spite of a bad ending. If audiences leave the theater confused or frustrated or angry or disappointed, the word-of-mouth will be negative, and the box office receipts will disappear.

So it is with your success story: the ending will make or break your ability to increase your revenue.

The Finish Line

In researching your case study, and interviewing your satisfied client or customer, ask, "When did you finally realize you had achieved your goal? What happened, exactly? Where were you? Who was with you? What did you do? How did others react? And what did that moment feel like?"

Then let us experience that moment of victory along with your hero.

Perhaps the hero of your case study received a check for five figures—more than he ever dreamed would be possible. Or maybe he was able to lift up his child for the first time without excruciating pain. Or perhaps the love of his life said yes to his proposal.

If you generalize these moments with statements like, "… and he finally achieved financial freedom," or "… and for the first time in a long time, he felt healthy," you will dissipate your buyers' emotional involvement rather than capitalize on it.

You've made your hero's goal vivid and specific. Now do the same with the climax.

It doesn't really matter what the moment was, as long as your description of it—the setting, the sounds, the sensations, the actions, and the deep emotions—is clear and vivid. Your readers and listeners don't just want a summary of your hero's success; they want to *feel* it.

The After Picture

Similarly, the more vivid your successful buyer's transformation, the more involving and enticing your story. And the more your hero's aftermath matches the dreams of your potential buyers, the more likely it is that they'll say yes to your offer.

Jump ahead to a moment a few months, or even years, after your hero achieved his goal. What was his life like then? How did it match what he longed for? What unexpected benefits did he receive from your product? How did his success affect others in his life—his family, his friends, his coworkers, and his customers?

Whatever problem your product solves, and whatever promise you make to your buyers, your hero's aftermath must show a life without that problem—a life with that promise fulfilled.

The specifics of your hero's aftermath won't match every buyer's exact dream. But the *meaning* conveyed by your hero's new life will.

Perhaps the successful subject of your case study now lives in a gorgeous log house, in a forest, beside a crystal blue lake, with a view of snow-capped mountains in the distance.

That may not be the dream of all your potential buyers. But if your product promises increased wealth, that home and that lake and that spectacular view represent what most of us deeply desire: financial independence, freedom, and a home surrounded by beauty and tranquility.

Your success story portrays a single individual who benefitted from your product or process or service. But because of the empathy you have created, and the emotional power of your hero's journey, the underlying message of your story is universal: *this could be you, this is what you can achieve, this can be your new life.*

It is only when your readers are convinced of this—thanks to the power of your story—that they will purchase whatever you are marketing.

You Have a First Draft!

Congratulations! Your story is written!

I know it isn't finished yet; there is still work to be done. But the hardest part is over. So, stop, congratulate yourself, and celebrate.

Now you get to begin a far more enjoyable process: *rewriting* your success story to maximize its potential, and to transform it from so-so to sensational.

CHAPTER 7

The Inner Journey

We all say we want to change.

But for the most part, we don't.

We only want our *circumstances* to change. We want to be richer, healthier, happier, more loved, and more fulfilled.

But we don't really want to change *ourselves*.

Unfortunately, accomplishing the first requires risking the second.

We're unlikely to achieve new levels of success if we hang onto our old levels of thought, behavior and emotion. But abandoning those familiar patterns means leaving our comfort zones and risking failure, loss, and rejection.

So, we'll go through the motions of change, then stop ourselves from any real transformation, because it's simply too scary.

From self-help books to motivational speakers to professional conferences to personal therapy, we'll spend bags of money to learn how to change. But the issue is almost never *how*. It's finding the courage to do what we already know.

In a long-ago series of *Pogo* comic strips, Albert Alligator wanted to lose weight.

"Eat less, exercise more," Porky Pine told him.

But instead Albert tried an amazing new diet that would help him shed pounds with no effort. When it failed, Porky said only, *"Eat less, exercise more."*

But Albert continued to try one miracle program after another without success. And each time one of his attempts failed, Porky would tell him, *"Eat less, exercise more."*

Albert never did follow Porky's advice. And he never lost any weight.

Deep down, Albert knew what he had to do to change. He just didn't want to do the work, preferring instead to simply *hope* his circumstances would magically transform.

This was probably true for the hero of your success story as well. And I guarantee it's true for your potential buyers. Because the truth is this: *the biggest obstacle you face in getting people to buy and use your product or process is that they're too afraid.*

Your customers won't admit this—they won't even realize it. Instead they'll say they're too poor or too busy or too smart or too dumb or too old or too young or too ugly for your product to work for them.

Or they'll do what we've all done: purchase the product and try it for a while, only to eventually abandon it for some new scheme that they think will lead to the change they desire.

At least you can make some money from this second group of buyers, because they'll pay for whatever you're selling just to give it a try, and to feel as if they're doing something positive. But they'll never become lasting customers, and they'll never bring you the satisfaction of truly transforming someone's life.

From Identity to Essence

So how do you use your success stories to help overcome your buyer's resistance to real change? The same way you convince them of your product's value: *by giving your potential buyers the emotional experience of courage and transformation.*

This is what a great movie does.

A hero begins the movie stuck in some way. He has been wounded in the past, and even though he thinks he has worked through that painful event or situation, it's still affecting his behavior. He has created an *identity*—a false self he presents to the world to protect himself from ever experiencing that pain again.

This identity—this artificial persona—is the emotional armor that keeps him feeling safe.

The problem is, it also keeps the hero from real success and transformation, because as long as he lives inside this identity, he can't change or grow, and he can't have what he truly wants.

Fulfillment for this character will only come when he finds the courage to leave his identity and live his *essence*—live the truth of the person he has the potential to become.

So as the hero pursues his visible goal, he is torn between feeling safe but stuck (in his identity), or feeling fulfilled but terrified (in his essence).

This tug-of-war is what is known as a character's *inner conflict*.

One of my favorite examples of this kind of character arc—this transformation from identity to essence—is in the film *Good Will Hunting*.

Will (Matt Damon) is a young man who as a child was repeatedly beaten by his father. As a result of this wound, he mistakenly believes that he must have deserved such punishment, and that if anyone were to see who he *really* is, they'd know he was worthless, and they'd abandon him.

So instead of revealing his math genius to anyone, he just hangs out with his townie friends, gets into fights, and works as a custodian at M.I.T.

This is his identity.

Then he meets Skylar (Minnie Driver), and he falls in love with her. But he can't bring himself to say that, or to commit to her, because to do so would mean leaving his protective identity and revealing his truth. She might see who he truly is, and risking that is unthinkable for Will. Letting her see his *essence* is just too terrifying. So, when she starts to get too close, he rejects her.

It is only with the help of the psychotherapist Sean (Robin Williams) that Will finds the courage to find his essence, reveal his intelligence, and express his love for Skylar. Only then does this hero find real fulfillment.

Revealing Your Hero's Fears

You can use these same storytelling principles in your case study by adding your hero's inner conflict to the visible obstacles you've already revealed in step four.

I purposely avoided discussing the principles of inner conflict in chapter 5, because including it in a success story is optional. Many blockbuster movies, and many very lucrative marketing stories, omit this element of the hero's journey. If the visible conflict in these stories is great enough, and if the story is compelling enough, audiences and customers will respond.

But revealing the hidden fears your hero faced as he pursued success will deepen the emotion of your stories, and will add greater empathy and conflict.

More important, your hero's inner journey can give your potential buyers the experience of overcoming the fears that they already feel about risking change and failure, and about taking a chance with your product.

In interviewing or researching the subject of your case study, explore the underlying fears that held her back in her journey: What was the hardest thing about this process? Did you ever feel stuck? Afraid? Were you ever tempted to give up? *Did* you give up at any point? Why? What went through your mind when you were tempted to stop, or whenever you missed a day of your new regimen?

Ask your potential hero about those internal and external voices that can sabotage our best intentions: What did you tell yourself that might have thwarted your progress? What did others say or do to set you back? What scared you most about following this new path? And did this remind you of any painful time in the past when you felt frightened or defeated?

Then find out how your subject found the courage to overcome these fears: How were you able to keep going? What did you tell yourself to avoid getting discouraged or defeated? What kind of support did you get from others? And if you were ever afraid, how did you overcome that fear?

Many of these questions are quite personal, so you'll need to build a level of trust to get your subject to open up in this way. But because you're talking to someone who was ultimately brave enough to succeed, she may be happy to share her wounds and fears in order to help others facing the same inner conflicts.

Your subject's spouse, or anyone else who helped your hero on her journey, will be a great source of material for exploring your hero's transformation from identity to essence. Your hero's loved ones are probably acutely aware of the fears that had to be overcome in order for her to achieve her goal.

Your case study doesn't have to reveal your hero's specific wounds from the past. What's most important is to reveal the blocks and fears she encountered as she pursued success—and how you, your program, and her support system helped her overcome them.

The fears your hero faced should match those that your potential buyers struggle with. It won't be too difficult, because we all fear the same thing: *the unknown.* We all plague ourselves with the same questions:

- What if trying this makes me look foolish? Greedy? Crazy?

- What if I'm wasting my money? What if I end up worse off than I am now?

- What if I fail, and I'm condemned to the life I'm now living? At least now I have my dreams for the future. If this new process doesn't work, and it proves my dreams were pointless, then what will I have to look forward to?

- What if I succeed? Will my friends and family see me the same way? Will I have to take on too much responsibility? Will I lose my sense of who I am?

You may also incorporate the fears and setbacks that *other* buyers or clients overcame when they found success with your product or process. Your case study isn't necessarily a single client's story—it can be a composite of truthful elements from several buyers' journeys.

If you are a consultant who works primarily with businesses, be aware that companies also possess identities that can prevent the change necessary to succeed. Perhaps they have been burned in the past by trying something new, or by hiring an outside consultant. Or perhaps they have been very successful in the past, and are now afraid of letting go of what has always worked so well for them.

Examples of companies stuck in their identities aren't hard to find. General Motors, IBM, Hewlett-Packard, Blockbuster, Hallmark, Sears, and that now-empty neighborhood mall that used to thrive— all have suffered losses or extinction because the companies couldn't let go of what they'd always done before. And for some, by the time they saw the light, they were too late to the game.

Consulting with or selling to these corporations requires you to convey—through both your stories and your work with them—that success will *always* mean stepping out of their comfort zones and into their fear of the unknown; to do otherwise will almost guarantee failure.

CHAPTER 8

Success Story Mastery

Rewriting isn't just a single pass through your story—it's an ongoing process of reading and re-reading, sharpening the story and increasing its emotional potential each time.

Writing Style Made Easy

With even a mention of improving the style of their prose, many storytellers get frightened and blocked, or give up altogether.

"I'm not a writer," they tell themselves. "I barely made it through English. I'm an awful speller. And I can't possibly compete with those writers who have big vocabularies, lots of education, and know how to weave magic with language. Who am I kidding?"

If this is you—if your stomach is in a knot, or you can feel yourself getting discouraged at just the thought of improving your writing, here's what you don't realize: *almost everything you think is required to become a good writer is incorrect.*

In fact, it's the opposite: what you assume to be the qualities of great writing will actually work against you.

The marks of a well-written story—and certainly of a well-written success story—are *simplicity* and *clarity.* Neither of these is achieved through big words, convoluted prose, or abstract ideas.

This is not to say that the works of literary masters like Melville or Faulkner or Joyce don't possess a lot of complexity and obliqueness—just ask anyone who had to slog through *Moby Dick* or *Ulysses* in college.

But would you want to read a how-to book or a marketing e-mail by any of those writers?

For our purposes, good stories are like good screenplays: fast, easy, and enjoyable to read.

Film stories move, enlighten, and persuade us by seducing us with vivid images and intriguing characters, then propelling us forward with emotionally involving action, conflict, and dialogue.

This is what you want your case studies to do. And you accomplish that goal by using your natural vocabulary, and speaking in your own voice.

Think of the last time you sat down with a friend to tell him about something that had happened to you. Did you stop yourself, worried your vocabulary wasn't sophisticated enough to keep him interested?

Did your friend start yawning or wander away because your prose was too simple?

I doubt it—in fact I'd wager that when you hear stories from others, your eyes start glazing over when the opposite happens—their narratives wander all over the place, or they try to sound smart or superior, and you simply can't follow what they're saying.

So, as you go through your completed case study, your goal is always to make it simpler and more personal. Your writing should have the feel of a conversation, where you're saying to your potential buyer, "Let me tell you what happened to this person I know...."

With that in mind, here are the elements of your story I suggest you review, edit and polish:

Tense

Imagine a case study that begins by describing the everyday life of a person suffering through his meaningless job at a collection agency:

"Sitting in his six-feet-by-six-feet cubicle, Henry stares blankly at the list of numbers on his computer screen, dreading the thought of phoning yet another person with a past-due credit card bill."

The above passage is written in present tense, which gives the story more immediacy. We feel like we're watching a movie that is unfolding right before our eyes.

But that same setup could just as easily have been written in past tense:

"As Henry sat inside his six-feet-by-six-feet cubical and stared blankly at the numbers on his computer screen, he dreaded the thought of phoning yet another person with a past-due credit card bill."

This version might be more appropriate for a case study, since the hero is someone who actually had this job in the past. Past tense is also more familiar to most readers and audiences, because it's used more frequently in both written and spoken stories.

The mistake would be to mix present and past tense. If the opening read, "Henry sits in his cubicle. He dreaded the thought of another phone call," the emotional potential of the sequence would be diminished, as readers tried to figure out why it sounded odd.

Choose whichever tense you believe is better for your story or feels more natural to you. Just never switch from one tense to the other within the story.

Details

A common weakness among all storytellers— screenwriters and novelists as well as marketers and corporate leaders and speakers—is the tendency to summarize.

When you write or tell a story, you are creating a movie in the mind of your readers or audiences. As they hear about your characters' lives and actions, they create mental images of what these characters look like, where they are, and what they're doing.

The more vivid those images, the more captivating and persuasive your story.

Surprisingly, the more specific and vivid the portrait of your hero's life (even if our own lives hardly resemble your hero's at all), the more universal your hero becomes. But the more generalized your description, the less we will identify with that character.

This means that the more detailed you are in describing settings and characters and action, the easier it will be for your readers and listeners to see the mental movie they're watching, and the more emotionally involved they will be.

Consider the setup of your story. You must introduce your hero living her everyday life, facing some kind of conflict that will increase empathy—a conflict your product will eventually solve. How can you make that setting, character, and action more specific and visible?

Let's suppose you are making a presentation about a system for increasing wealth, and the subject of your success story is a woman who was in financial trouble and used your product to multiply her income.

You might begin your story by saying, "Catherine was a single mother struggling with a recent financial setback."

This will certainly give your audience a sense of her everyday life, and they'll feel some degree of empathy for her. But the picture they envision will be fuzzy and vague, because you've summarized her situation.

Imagine introducing that same hero with this scene:

"Catherine was bundled up in her bathrobe as she sat in the kitchen of her tiny one-bedroom apartment. The rickety card table in front of her was loaded with stacks of unopened envelopes. As her two young daughters devoured yet another meal of Spaghetti-Os, she desperately tried to separate the bills that had to be paid right away from the ones that could be put off for another month."

Aren't you immediately more involved with this woman? Feeling sorrier for her? Caring more about her?

Or let's say your product is a vitamin supplement to improve health. Won't describing the way your client was winded after climbing the stairs with his young son be more vivid and powerful than simply saying he had asthma, or was out of shape?

Don't get carried away and let your descriptive passages continue endlessly. Limit yourself to two or three details each for setting, character, or action.

The illustration above mentions the hero's apartment, her bathrobe, a card table, stacks of bills, separating them, and Spaghetti-O's—six vivid elements to create images of the setting, the hero, her children, and her action. But it doesn't continue talking about peeling paint or her slippers or what her two girls were wearing or what the dishes looked like or what kind of pen she was holding. The six selected items are sufficient to give a snapshot of the scene without the passage going on and on.

Your descriptions should also convey as much about your hero's *inner* life as possible. Do they give us a glimpse of how your hero was stuck? Of his fears throughout the story? Of his feelings of fulfillment after his eventual success and transformation? Of the ways those around him were transformed as well?

We don't just see images; we interpret them. The more your descriptions lead to a deeper understanding of your hero, the more powerful they will be.

Look also for places where you are adding your

own commentary regarding what happened to your hero, rather than simply telling the story.

Saying, "Charles was discouraged," reveals your interpretation of what was going on. But saying, "Every morning Charles crawled out of bed and put his feet on the threadbare carpet, wondering if this would be the day that his life might change," allows readers to draw their own conclusions.

Of course, any marketing tool can include summaries and commentary describing the product you're pitching. But the story portion of the ad is built on details of action, description and dialogue.

Dialogue

Take a look at the following paragraph:

> When Jim told his wife how discouraged he was with his health problems, and that he worried things would never improve, she told him not to lose faith, and that they would find some way to help him get better.

This isn't bad—it already includes some key elements of a success story. We get a picture of these two characters and how they are stuck. We empathize with them, we have a sense of their problem and goal, we're rooting for Jim to get healthier, and we're curious about how that can happen.

But compare it to this passage:

Jim looked tearfully into his wife's eyes. "I just don't think things will ever get any better."

"Don't worry," she told him as she gently took his hand. "We're going to find a way to beat this."

Which version is more emotionally involving? Which creates a more vivid picture of what's happening? Which makes you more eager to keep reading?

Dialogue is a powerful tool for drawing your readers into your success stories. Quoting your characters—using their exact words—makes your stories more immediate, more vivid, more revealing, and more involving.

Just make certain your dialogue feels real:

- *Does it mimic the way people actually talk?*

- *Do your characters use the kind of slang we're used to hearing in real life?*

- *Is their vocabulary appropriate for their backgrounds, personalities, and professions?*

- *Do they speak naturally, or do they "announce" their desires and feelings?*

- *Do they speak easily and loosely, the way people who have known each other for some time do, or do they repeatedly address each other by name?*

After you've added dialogue to a story, read it out loud. Does it sound like something you might actually hear people say? If not, keep playing with it until it feels natural.

Professionalism

Now we come to the dreaded rules of *spelling, grammar,* and *punctuation.*

I have friends and clients who are very successful Internet marketers, and who don't worry about typos or incorrect word usage. They figure that mistakes are beside the point, and that whatever they write, appropriate or not, is an honest expression of who they are.

I disagree.

As you know by now, my approach to a story is all about creating as much emotional involvement for your readers as you can. And any time a reader encounters a misspelled word or a misplaced comma, he's pulled out of the story. Instead of remaining inside the world you've created, he's now concentrating on the words themselves, wondering whether what you wrote is correct or not.

It's not as if your potential buyer will say, "If this guy doesn't know how to spell, I won't do business with him." But he might be so distracted by the errors in your prose that he loses interest in the story you're telling (and he may subconsciously begin to question your level of professionalism).

To correct these mistakes, begin by spell checking every document you post.

Then do a search of words that are often confused because they sound the same but have different meanings and uses, starting with *there* (a place), *their* (a possessive), and *they're* (a contraction for *they are*). Search *its* and *it's* as well. And *lose* versus *loose*.

Your word processing program should also catch some grammatical errors. And if you're really grammar and punctuation challenged, have a friend or copy editor who's good at those elements proofread your story for you.

Here are two other very common weaknesses to avoid:

Unnecessary Repetition

A key way to avoid overlong or meandering stories is to eliminate unnecessary repetition. As you reread your story, do you find it circling back to make the same point over and over? Are you repeating words or phrases—sometimes within the same paragraph—rather than adding some variety to your prose?

If your case study is broken into sections to be e-mailed over a number of days, then it's a good idea to remind the reader of where the story left off in the previous e-mail, and perhaps to reiterate the key points you've made so far.

Then move on to something new. Make certain your hero takes new actions, faces new obstacles, and that new principles are revealed with each successive sequence or e-mail.

Irrelevance

Remove any situations or sequences that are unnecessary or irrelevant to your story, and to your hero's visible goal. Perhaps you've created an emotional encounter between your hero and his daughter. But if this doesn't in some way connect to his outer motivation—his visible goal in the story—then it should be deleted, no matter how touching it might be.

The principles above are all pretty basic and universal. In the next chapter, I want to share some special storytelling tricks and techniques that add magic to Hollywood movies—tricks you can easily employ in your own storytelling as well.

CHAPTER 9

Hollywood Magic

Working with filmmakers and storytellers for several decades, I've picked up some of the key tools used in movies and TV shows to enthrall audiences. You can use these same tricks of the trade to maximize the power of your own stories as well.

Structural Tools and Techniques

In addition to the overall structure of your success stories—the six steps, in sequence—several additional movie techniques will help you decide what should happen, and when:

> ➤ **The Ticking Clock**

When your hero says, "I want to get in shape," a goal is revealed, but it's vague, undefined, and hard to visualize. "I want to win a triathlon," is far more involving, because we can picture your hero puffing along, or crossing a finish line, exhausted but fulfilled.

But "I have to be ready to complete the Ironman Triathlon in three months!" is stronger still. Not only is it more specific and vivid, it gives your hero a time limit.

Introducing a deadline into your story greatly increases our emotional involvement, because the conflict is now even greater. A race against time raises the stakes—and the obstacles—for your hero.

A client who, with your help, made $30,000 can be the basis for a solid success story. But imagine a client who, with your help, had to make $30,000 *before the bank took away her home.* Now you have the makings of an unforgettable success story about a client who was able to do the impossible.

➤ Curiosity

Readers like puzzles. When we read stories, we like to wonder why and how the events occurred or how the hero was able to succeed. We don't want everything presented so flatly and in such an expository way that there's no mystery to it, and nothing to keep us turning the page.

Don't give everything away up front, and don't explain everything as soon as it occurs. And never give away the ending before it happens.

Which are you more likely to read—a story about someone living in her dream house, or a story about someone who was desperate to buy her dream house? I'm guessing you'd pick the one where you don't immediately know how the hero reached the desired finish line.

Imagine creating a success story with these beats, in sequence:

- Your hero got a notice in the mail that she knew would turn her life upside down...

- She carried it in her pocket for two days, afraid to face the reality of what it meant...

- She came to you as a consultant because she was desperate to know how to deal with what the letter said...

- She handed you the letter, and only then did you (and now your readers) realize that she had inherited $200,000, and she had no idea how to handle that kind of windfall.

Isn't that a much more seductive buildup than to open your story saying, "I once had a client who inherited $200,000?"

> **Anticipation**

When we read or hear stories, just as when we watch movies, we want to try to guess what's going to happen next. It's not just the action of the moment that enthralls us; it's the anticipation of what's coming.

We imagine what will happen when the hero encounters the villain, when the hero and heroine finally kiss, or when the cops realize the hero just robbed a bank.

Creating that anticipation in your success story increases your buyers' involvement in the same way. Get them guessing what's about to happen, and they'll keep reading or listening.

Instead of saying, "Then our team of consultants began working with his employees," try "They had no idea what to expect the first day our team of consultants arrived at their warehouse."

See how this very small adjustment will have your potential clients wondering, and imagining, what might happen next? Their involvement in your story increases, and the emotional experience of working with your company becomes even stronger.

➤ Superior Position

My favorite Hollywood technique for creating anticipation is to give the audience *superior position.* This simply means that the audience knows something the characters in the movie don't know.

We learn who the killer is, or that the demon is lurking inside the house, or that the cheating wife's husband is on his way home from work—all before the hero knows this.

In your case study, perhaps you reveal in the setup that the hero doesn't yet realize he is about to lose his job. Or in the action and conflict steps, he is unaware that his biggest competitor is about to release a new product almost identical to his.

As soon as you let us in on the secret, we start anticipating what will happen when your hero learns what we already know.

> ## ➤ Surprise

Horror movies always contain at least one moment when the demon unexpectedly leaps out and the audience lets out a scream.

It's the same in the success stories you tell. As much as your readers enjoy trying to guess what will happen next, sometimes we want to be knocked over by something unexpected.

Perhaps, just when we think your hero is on the verge of victory, you'll say, "And just as he smiled in satisfaction over a job well done, his web site crashed, and his entire marketing campaign along with it."

Your buyers are thrown off balance, wondering what just happened. But they certainly won't stop reading or listening, as you give one more example of how your product helped your successful client overcome some major setback.

➤ Credibility

One of your biggest concerns in marketing a product or service is that the amazing results you promise will sound fictitious—that your prospects will think you're just making things up to get a sale.

Here's a great technique for combating issues of credibility for your potential buyers: *voice their skepticism before they have a chance to think it.*

During the uncertainty portion of step two, as you relate how you tried to convince the hero of the story to try your product or service, have your hero say to you, "That's unbelievable," or, "That sounds too good to be true," or, "Do you really expect me to believe that?"

Then you (or whoever recommended your company to your satisfied client) can reply, "I thought the same thing when I first heard about (insert your name here). So, I did some research of my own, and everyone I spoke to reported the same results—or better!"

You won't necessarily use all of these subtler techniques in a single speech or case study. Just weave in the most appropriate ones for whatever success story you're telling, and it will become even more involving—and persuasive.

Openings

In previous chapters, I presented the six simple steps in chronological order, which is the way most stories in or outside of Hollywood are told. This is why I logically began with the setup, because it reveals your hero's everyday life before he begins the journey that leads him to your product or service. But there are three alternative openings Hollywood employs to seduce audiences—openings that sometimes might strengthen the emotional impact of your own stories as well.

1. The Aftermath Opening

You may want to begin at the end of your success story, by painting a vivid picture of your hero's everyday life *after* using your product or process.

With this aftermath opening, we first meet your hero already living the life she dreamed of—the same life your potential buyer longs for. Your hero is healthy, or wealthy, or in a loving relationship, or winning a competition, or whatever other state of being your product promises.

This can be a very powerful method for seducing your potential buyers. "That's what I want!" they think. "I'd give anything to live like that." Then they keep reading to find out how to make that fantasy a reality.

Once you've revealed your hero's aftermath, you insert some version of the words, "But it wasn't always that way for her. Just a short time ago she was…" And then you flash back to the setup, before your hero discovered the path to success that your product or your coaching provided.

Once your hero arrives at the climax, you return to the aftermath to briefly remind your readers of the rewards your hero earned—which they can, too, if they purchase whatever you're marketing.

2. The Huge Obstacle Opening

Here you open your case study in the middle of the story—just as your hero is facing some major obstacle, setback or threat. This might be the crisis that moved your hero to action initially, or it might be a later conflict for your hero.

But instead of immediately resolving this conflict and revealing how your hero overcame such a huge obstacle, you leave your readers in suspense. You flash back to the setup, and begin telling the story chronologically, just as you would with an aftermath opening.

Huge obstacle openings employ three of the powerful techniques I revealed earlier in this chapter: curiosity (we wonder how the hero will overcome this obstacle), superior position (we know the disaster that awaits the hero, but he does not), and anticipation (we're thinking about the major conflict that awaits the hero).

These openings can be seen on a daily basis on television. Crime and action series frequently open with their heroes in life threatening, no-way-of-surviving situations. As they face certain death, a title card appears, something like…

SIX HOURS EARLIER

…and then the camera dissolves to a scene in the past, when everything was nice and calm. Then a body is discovered or a crisis is revealed, and we're off to the races.

Because of the immediate conflict, this style of opening creates a high level of emotion, and will keep your readers scrolling ahead, or your audiences on the edge of their seats.

3. The Prologue Opening

You might also consider opening your case study with a scene from the distant past, before you move to the setup and your hero's everyday life.

Let's say your speech opens like this:

"When she was ten years old, living in a Baltimore housing project, Janet saw a picture of the Eiffel

Tower in a magazine. From that moment on, she had a fantasy of someday traveling to Paris herself.

"But as Janet grew older, and time passed, money was always scarce, bills never seemed to get paid, and her dream remained just that.

"Then one day, as she completed working a double shift waiting tables, she overheard one customer telling another about all the extra money he'd been making in his spare time…"

Your speech would then reveal how Janet heard this stranger's story about using your system, and how she then went on to make money herself using the same system, until finally she was able to fulfill that lifelong fantasy of seeing the Eiffel Tower.

The first paragraph—your description of ten-year-old Janet—is the prologue of your story. The description of adult Janet, working as a waitress, is the setup, just as in any success story.

A prologue opening allows you to create even more empathy with your hero—and more conflict to your story—as we identify with the pain she felt in the past, or her subsequent discouragement and defeat as her hopes and dreams were shattered.

This an excellent approach if you want to explore the inner journey for your hero. The prologue reveals a wounding experience in the past that led to your hero's emotional fear—one that she will have to face and overcome to achieve her visible goal.

In Janet's story above, you might go on to reveal how she was reluctant to hire you or your company because she had been disappointed so many times. She became afraid to pursue her dreams because the thought of another failure was simply too painful.

Since this is a very common inner conflict for potential buyers, Janet's inner journey will resonate with your audiences, and allow you to show how your approach can help them overcome their own fears, and to achieve their own success.

Play around with these three opening styles to see if any is appropriate for whatever success story you're telling. The goal of each opening is always the same: to seduce your audiences with an emotionally involving scene in order to capture their attention—and emotion—and force them to keep listening.

Illustrations

Movies enthrall us with their images. It becomes easy for us to believe the events are happening to us because they're right in front of our eyes.

Screenwriters and fiction writers (unless they're graphic novelists or children's book authors) can't use images to involve their readers. Illustrations are not allowed. These writers must create captivating stories using only words.

But if you're a speaker or a blogger or a marketer, you don't have that same restriction. Success stories in speeches, posts, e-mails, and sales pitches can include photographs and illustrations.

With permission from the subjects of your success stories, you can show snapshots or slides of your heroes, their families, and their surroundings. Audiences and readers will actually see the home where your hero was living in poverty, or the office cubicle where he slaved away, or the mountain where he used to ski before suffering the physical setback that your product will treat.

Perhaps best of all, you can show pictures or videos of your hero's aftermath—the panoramic view looking out over the ocean from his family's new home, or the luxury car he now drives, or the distant land to which he traveled, or the trophy he won after using your training method.

Or we can see for ourselves the new, modern facilities where the company you coached now resides, or the joyful employees reaping the benefits of their newfound success. This is just one more way to make the success you're promising come alive for your potential buyer.

CHAPTER 10

Autobiographical Stories

An important part of making a presentation is building rapport and trust with your audiences and potential clients. They are far more likely to follow the advice of (and pay money to) someone they know, and with whom they empathize, than with a stranger who simply makes a great sales pitch.

This is why you always want at least one success story in your arsenal where you are the hero.

For most of the speakers, marketers, and business leaders I work with, telling autobiographical stories is a frightening prospect.

"Who would want to hear about me?" they ask. "I'm not a celebrity. I've never suffered, and I've never done anything special. It'll just be boring!"

What they fail to recognize is that most successful movies (other than a few big superhero films) are about everyday heroes, who start out as unremarkable and unheralded people until they're forced to face some crisis.

Consider recent Oscar nominees *Spotlight, Bridge of Spies, The Big Short, Room, La La Land, Manchester By the Sea,* and *Hidden Figures.* The heroes of these films, whether real or fictional, were all fairly ordinary people living mundane lives before they were confronted with opportunities or crises that launched their journeys.

We don't root for these characters because they are unique or powerful, or because they have to save the world, but because we empathize with them, and we're emotionally invested in their success at whatever goals they're pursuing.

In the same way, your readers and audiences don't connect with you because you're a superhero. *They identify with you because you have experienced the same kinds of pain, and longed for the same kinds of success and happiness, that they do.*

An even bigger concern about autobiographical stories—particularly among speakers and presenters—is that making oneself the hero of a success story is egomaniacal. "I can't talk about myself," they say. "It'll seem like I'm boasting, or superior, or full of myself."

This worry is well founded. We've all sat through speeches by people with "I" trouble: "*I* did this, and then *I* did this, and now *I'm* rich and *I'm* happy and you should do what *I* did."

This is an approach you should avoid.

Instead, when you tell your own success story, begin by sharing the pain you were experiencing before you began your journey—just as you would for the setup of any hero. Reveal your fears, your shortcomings, and your failures—not simply to create empathy, but to convey to your readers that you don't see yourself as anything special or gifted.

As you pursue your goal in the story, reveal the difficulties you had and the setbacks you experienced and the times you wanted to give up.

Then—and this is most important—*give credit for your success to others.* Talk about the mentors who guided you, or the loved ones who stood by you, or the words of wisdom and inspiration that kept you going. And of course, reveal the qualities of the product or process you're promoting that empowered you to overcome the obstacles you faced.

But what if you had no mentors? Or what about the times you came up with ideas on your own, or overcame your own obstacles?

This is when you need to reveal *how* you came up with these brilliant ideas and methods—the ones that distinguish your product from all the others. So instead of saying, "Aren't I brilliant!" you're laying out the work that *preceded* your inspiration or courage.

Show how your discovery or insight arrived in a moment of defeat or despair: "I was ready to throw in the towel and go back to my old, miserable job. But then I thought, 'What if I gave it one more shot and did this (your new idea)?' So, I tried it and it worked!"

Telling your story in this way increases our empathy (because of your pain), raises the stakes (you were about to give up), leaves us in suspense (anticipating what happened next), and makes it seem as if your brilliance was a gift from the gods (rather than because you're so special and unique).

There is one quality, however, that you *are* allowed to brag about: *hard work*.

Talk about how, after years of studying dozens of systems for success, or after decades of expensive education or expensive coaching or career experience, you were able to create your product or service. When your target market hears this, they're not thinking, "Isn't she full of herself." They're thinking, "If I hire her or buy from her, it will save me from having to do all that hard work myself!" And they'll be eager to send you money.

Remember, in a well-told success story, audiences empathize with the hero and take the journey along with that character. They participate in his success as they experience it with him.

So it will be with your autobiographical success story. You are not setting yourself apart from your audience by making yourself superior. You are uniting with them to achieve success *together.*

One final principle, which takes us back to the beginning: when you tell a story about how successful you were at helping someone else, make that *client* the hero, not yourself.

Sure, you did a wonderful job of turning someone's life around, and of course you want to make certain your readers get the point, and are so impressed that they'll immediately want to hire you. But they will be more likely to do that if you create empathy with your successful customer (who was in a situation similar to the one they're in), rather than shining the spotlight on yourself (with whom your audience may have little in common).

In other words, in illustrating your own expertise, stick with success stories as outlined in all the previous chapters, and use autobiographical stories sparingly, and appropriately.

As you tell more and more stories in your speeches and e-mails, you will most likely develop several autobiographical stories that recount different times in your life and career where you learned the principles and methods and values that led to your product or service. This is fine. The greater the number of persuasive stories you have to choose from, the greater your success will be.

CHAPTER 11

Beyond Success Stories

The tools and principles for creating powerful success stories can be applied to other stories, situations, and contexts, always with the goal of eliciting greater emotion, and enticing potential buyers or clients to purchase your products or services, or employ your principles and methods.

Mentor Stories

Success stories about people who have guided you or inspired you will probably *not* directly involve whatever you're selling. These are not people who have used your product or hired you as a consultant; if they had, you would create the kind of success story we've been discussing since chapter 1.

The heroes of these stories are either mentors who guided you, or people unknown to you in real life, but whose words or deeds you learned about through books or movies or speeches.

With a mentor story, the successes achieved, or

the wisdom imparted, *conveys the philosophy behind your product or process or call to action*. These heroes might have discovered a fact or a principle that led you to develop your product, or that formed a cornerstone of your business or your system. Or perhaps they simply exhibited attitudes or behaviors that you replicated in your own life, and doing so was a critical component of your success.

However they touched you, six-step success stories about them will touch your readers and audiences in the same way.

I sometimes term these *Wise Leader* stories, because they focus on heroes whose words or actions offer us models for how we might live our lives—or at least how we might look at our feelings and actions in new, empowering ways.

Wise leader heroes are ubiquitous in books and speeches and pleas for donations. The *Chicken Soup for the Soul* franchise is built on this kind of story, as are most sermons and telethons.

These stories can educate, inspire, motivate, and move readers or audiences or employees or congregations to take action. Captivating mentor stories can also be an important addition to a marketing campaign or sales pitch, by either revealing the mission statement and ethical principles of an organization, or by conveying the psychology or philosophy behind a service or process.

Failure Stories

Not all persuasive stories need to be success stories. You can also move others to take action by revealing the cost of inaction or of choosing the wrong solution to their problems.

This can be a great device in autobiographical stories. Reveal a time in your life or your business when you desperately wanted to achieve your goal, and you were certain you had found the path to victory. Then show how the products or the methods you chose *failed* to achieve the success you longed for.

The aftermath of this well-told failure story will portray the end of your journey, where you were once again stuck just the way you were in the setup (or worse). This dismal after picture will reveal the *lesson* that you learned through failure—a lesson that led you to the right solution to your problem—the product or system you are now recommending.

Failure stories can also be incorporated into a regular success story. Before revealing how your client or customer achieved her goal using your product, tell a story about how she failed when she used your competitor's. The steps she took in her failure story should be the opposite of those she then took when she began following your approach.

Not only will you give your potential buyers the emotional experience of success with your product, you'll precede it by letting them experience the failure that will ensue when they make any *other* choice. Your message is now doubly powerful.

A variation of this is the rich man/poor man approach. Lay out two intertwined stories of someone who repeatedly succeeds using your system, and another who repeatedly fails by refusing to do things "correctly." Each step these two heroes take will push readers toward your approach, and away from the alternatives.

Internet marketing legend André Chaperon uses this principle brilliantly with his fictional Internet marketers Frank and Matt (http://frankvsmatt. com/). He uses Frank to illustrate all of the common mistakes entrepreneurs make in pursuing profits, while Matt makes all the right choices that lead to success and wealth.

By repeatedly comparing Frank's failure stories with Matt's success stories, André's readers are taught the principles of his proven approach. And because they of course want to be like successful Matt and not failure Frank, they are drawn to André's products at the same time.

Soap Opera Sequences

An even bigger contribution André has made to the world of Internet marketing is with the concept of soap opera sequences. This is the method responsible for his greatest successes, and one of the things that sets him apart from most gurus in the Internet marketing world.

Since André is the master of this form of storytelling and marketing, I won't even attempt to delve into the key elements of soap opera sequences, particularly when you can learn the process so much better and more clearly through his own website: http://tinylittlebusinesses.com/.

But the underlying story principles involved are completely consistent with what you have learned about success stories and the six simple steps: *elicit emotion in your readers by portraying empathetic characters who face compelling conflicts as they pursue clearly defined goals.*

André's SOS system skillfully adds the power of *anticipation* and *curiosity* to this formula. Instead of a single marketing e-mail, he creates a series of e-mails (much like episodes of a soap opera) that contain some kind of cliffhanger or unresolved question or situation at the end of each one. This entices potential buyers to continue reading, and sustains their emotional involvement with each successive chapter.

André's products are gradually introduced as his series of stories continues. By the time his subscribers encounter the actual offers, they are fully engaged—and eager to buy.

If you watch episodic TV (and I watch a *lot* of episodic TV), you'll notice that each commercial break follows something awful happening, or the realization that something awful is *about* to happen, or some new revelation that tells the audience, "Wait a minute—this isn't over yet. Don't leave now or you'll miss what's coming next!"

The number one fear of episodic TV writers and producers is that viewers will flip to another program during a commercial. Their objective is always to make the audience eager to come back to the episode. Since emotion grows out of conflict, that means leaving audiences hanging at moments of crisis, or with new, even more impossible objectives.

It's the same with a series of soap opera sequence e-mails. The hero of the story faces a challenge, and in the e-mail that follows, readers will find out how he overcame that obstacle, what happened next, and what crisis he will have to overcome in the *next* e-mail. Or perhaps the author of the e-mail series simply says, "Then I discovered a powerful secret. And I'll tell you all about it next time..."

Either way, it keeps readers coming back for more, and brings them closer to clicking the *order now* button.

You can employ this same principle if you're a speaker. Begin your speech with a story, but interrupt the story at a crisis point for your hero. Then move into the main content of your speech—the themes, principles, methods, or data you're presenting to your audience. Come back to your story repeatedly through the course of your speech, or simply conclude the story at the end. Either approach to breaking up your story will increase your audiences' involvement as they wait to hear the outcome for your hero.

Testimonials

One of the most powerful ways of luring potential customers is with testimonials. Having others say how great you (or your product) are will often make the difference between a sale and a lost prospect.

Since they both involve convincing the marketplace of the effectiveness of your product, think of testimonials as success stories in miniature.

In other words, apply success story principles to the testimonials you request. Look for ways to build character, desire, and conflict into the praise others give for your product or service.

Consider this testimonial:

Mitchell is an amazing coach! He makes sure you walk your walk and talk your talk. With his help, I was able to strengthen our brand and do more of what I love without increasing my workload or raising my overhead. His one-on-one sessions zeroed in on exactly what I should promise my clients. Even my staff said how much more positive I was, and how inspired they were by my enthusiasm. Our revenue and client list increased dramatically within just a few months. You won't be sorry you hired Mitchell! I highly recommend him.

Clearly this client loved working with Mitchell, was happy with the result, and strongly recommends him to others. This no doubt moves people closer to hiring him.

The problem is, it's not very specific—or emotional.

This former client had lots of positive feelings about working with Mitchell, but his testimonial doesn't allow us to *experience* those feelings ourselves. We don't feel any particular empathy for the client, nor do we have a clear picture of what the process of working with Mitchell was like, because it is sorely lacking in specifics.

The testimonial does reveal an outcome: increased revenue. But without defining that result more specifically, and without a vivid, attractive aftermath that holds more universal appeal, the persuasive power of this testimonial is limited.

So, let's see how we might use Six Step Success Story principles to turn this into a testimonial that would lead to much better results:

> *Mitchell's unique process is amazing! For more than a year, I had been working endless hours trying to build my business evaluating and training middle management executives. But my client list was flatlining, and I was still struggling to make ends meet. I was beginning to think the life I had dreamed of simply wasn't for me.*
>
> *Then I heard Mitchell on a podcast, and his approach to achieving success sounded so simple and logical, I decided to take a chance. As he took me through his unique style of*

questions, exercises, and tough-love support, he forced me to see how I wasn't leveraging my greatest strengths, and how the steps I'd been taking to ensure my success were actually getting in my way.

After just two strategy sessions I was able to book my biggest (and highest paying) client, and in the six months since, working far fewer hours than I used to, my consulting revenue has doubled—and I'm actually having fun!

Notice as well how the testimonial touches on all the same steps as any well-told success story: 1) struggled to make ends meet, 2) heard a podcast and hired Mitchell to increase revenue, 3) got coaching, 4) had to overcome past mistakes, 5) signed biggest client, and 6) doubled revenue and more fun.

And because of the specific details that weren't in the first version, we feel more empathy for the speaker, we have a clearer sense of Mitchell's approach, and results, and we are able to picture—and experience— the long-term rewards Mitchell's client achieved.

Success story principles can even be applied to much shorter testimonials.

"The best product money can buy," is a strong recommendation—particularly if it comes from someone with name recognition—and it contains no story element at all. But when a short testimonial at least describes some specific element of the problem overcome, the goal achieved, or the aftermath, it will be even stronger.

Will Smith generously provided me with a testimonial when the latest edition of my book *Writing Screenplays That Sell* was released. His quote (which I have shamelessly included in just about every marketing campaign I've done since) simply states:

> *No one is better than Michael Hauge at finding what is most authentic in every moment of a story.*
>
> — Will Smith, star of *Men in Black, I Am Legend, Ali, The Pursuit of Happyness, Suicide Squad*

The strength of this testimonial—beyond having Will's name attached to it—is that it conveys a goal that I was able to help him achieve: creating a story that is completely authentic.

The specificity of the quote gives the sense that this client actually had this experience working with me, and that anyone reading the testimonial will have that experience if they hire me as well.

The One-Sentence Story

Even when you have only a minute—or a single sentence—to pitch your company or your product or your service, you can begin seducing potential customers by incorporating success story principles.

I often get invited to speak about story principles at corporate breakfast meetings—weekly or monthly meals where a group of business executives get together to network and help each other market themselves.

These events almost always begin the same way: going clockwise around the conference table as participants introduce themselves.

These self-descriptions always follow the same Name–Title–Company–Brand template:

"My name is Bill, and I'm the COO for Acme Insurance. We specialize in consolidated plans for seven-figure service companies."

I sometimes commandeer these tedious and near-meaningless introductions and ask members of the meeting to do something a bit different.

"When you introduce yourself," I tell them, "instead of giving us your title or telling us what your company does, tell us—in just one sentence— something specific you've done for a client or customer, and how it benefitted them."

After some skeptical grumbling—and occasional dirty looks—they give it a try:

"My name is Charles, and my agency recently saved a bottling plant $400,000 by helping them consolidate their executive insurance plans into a new company package."

"Hi, I'm Nancy Lynn, I'm a chiropractor, and I helped a new patient get rid of her back pain after three office visits."

"Good morning, I'm Jimmie, and I'm with Sonora Consultants. Last year we assisted a potato chip company with their West Coast expansion into six new states."

An executive at one of these meetings once admitted that even though he had been attending for more than a year, this was the first time he actually understood what it was that the other members did.

Why does this matter? Well, beyond creating a much greater camaraderie within a group, these breakfasts are designed as a means of connecting with new prospects through referrals.

But how good a recommendation can one attendee give another if he only has a vague idea of what that person's company does, or what the benefits might be?

Even these mini-stories are far more emotional, and far more powerful at elevating success, than flat recitations of name, title, and job description.

(And by the way, did you notice that this story about corporate breakfast meetings is also a not-very-subtle example of an autobiographical success story, with myself as the hero? Can you spot the setup, crisis, pursuit, conflict, climax, and aftermath? They're all there.)

CHAPTER 12

Taking Your Own Hero's Journey

One of my favorite lines in one of my favorite films, *Postcards from the Edge* (adapted by Carrie Fisher from her novel), occurs when the hero Suzanne (played by Meryl Streep) proclaims, "I don't want life to imitate art; I want life to *be* art."

Believe it or not, when you create a story, even a marketing story, you're creating art. You are imitating real life, in spoken or written form, in order to move, enlighten, and inspire your readers and audiences. You are connecting with others in a way that will help them solve their problems and achieve greater feelings of growth and happiness and fulfillment.

In other words, their lives will imitate—or at least learn from—the art you have created.

But as you've gone through this book and learned this process and created your success stories, you may also have discovered something else: that *a well-told story has the power to change lives, including the life of the storyteller.*

When you first encountered this book or this process, you were in the setup of this journey. You were stuck in some way, prevented from moving forward toward greater success because you lacked one of the tools you needed.

Then something happened that forced you onto this new path—a financial crisis, or the realization that the status quo for your business was simply no longer acceptable, or simply a recommendation from a friend that learning to tell effective stories could improve your marketing skills and increase your revenue.

So, you began to ask questions. "What should I do? What will make the difference? Where can I find the solution?"

Learning about this book led to more questions: "Who is this guy Michael Hauge? What is he asking me to do? Will it work? Is it worth my time? My money? Can I even do this?"

Perhaps you even acquired this book and skimmed through it, asking more questions to help you decide if you wanted to give this new method a try.

This, as you probably already know, is the stage where most people give up and move on to the next expert or the next method or the next product that they hope will change their lives. (If you doubt that, just take a look at all the unused programs and unfinished business or self-help books on almost any executive's or speaker's or marketer's shelves— including your own.)

But if you've made it all the way to this chapter, it means you actually took the leap, defined your goal, and have begun incorporating success stories into your marketing and speaking.

You moved forward, finding the tenacity and courage to keep at it in spite of the obstacles and setbacks you encountered.

And as you begin enjoying all the rewards of what you're doing, stop to remember how hard—and how scary—this journey seemed at the beginning.

Perhaps you started by thinking, "I'm no storyteller—I'm just not built that way. I know this is going to be impossible."

Even if those weren't your thoughts, I know that as you began creating your success stories, you encountered moments of doubt and discouragement and frustration and fear.

So, what was it that scared you about pursuing and achieving the success you wanted? What were you resisting, what made you uncomfortable, what steps did you tell yourself you couldn't possibly do, because, "That's just not me?"

Were you told you were no good at writing in school, and you didn't want to subject your storytelling to that same kind of judgment and criticism?

Did you say to yourself, "I've never been much of a storyteller?"

Were you always taught that it's not nice to brag, so you thought telling your own success story would be shameless boasting?

Or are you a "facts and figures" type of person who saw all this as too emotional and touchy-feely, or too esoteric for high-level executives?

Whatever your resistance was, whatever identity you had to leave behind, you ultimately found the strength and support to face those inner conflicts and keep moving.

In other words, you stopped asking yourself, "How can I not be afraid?" and instead asked the far more empowering question, *"Am I willing to be afraid?"*

This, as much as any other principle you've learned or technique you've used, is the reason you were finally able to present your success stories to your audiences and readers and potential buyers.

Never forget this. Because from now on, the more often you visualize and internalize the moments of perseverance and power and success and fulfillment you experienced during this process, the stronger and more courageous you will be when you begin your next pursuit, and your next and your next.

And in that way, you will continue to be the hero of your own journey.

AND NOW...

I hope you have found this book helpful, and that you're already using stories more powerfully, and more successfully, in your presentations and your marketing. But please don't stop now.

Keep sharpening your storytelling skills through articles and blogs and books and practice, practice, practice.

Keep adding more success stories—both case studies and autobiographical stories—to your arsenal.

Keep applying these story principles to your testimonials, your websites, and your social media pages, along with your speeches, e-mails, sales calls, and blogs.

And one request: please e-mail me at Contact@ StoryMastery.com to tell me the storytelling challenges you feel or encounter, what you found helpful in this book, and how I might be of help. I read every e-mail personally, and I would love to hear from you, and to someday work with you or your company to help you connect with your audiences and clients and customers more powerfully and effectively.

Thanks for taking this journey with me.

Stay in your essence!

APPENDIX I

Summary of the Six Steps

Preparation: Find Your Hero

Research those who have succeeded using the principles you are presenting, the product you are marketing, or the service you are promoting until you can select the appropriate case study and hero for your story.

- Search your own past, stories you have read or heard, testimonials

- Look at successful clients and customers

- Research and interview several possible subjects/heroes for your story

- Include spouses and loved ones

- Use questionnaires if interviews aren't possible

Step One: The Setup

Show the everyday life your hero was living

before he heard about or began using your product or service. This before picture will create empathy for your hero, so your readers and audiences experience his success on an emotional level.

- Give a snapshot of your hero's everyday life
- Create empathy
  - ❖ Sympathy—undeserved misfortune
  - ❖ Worry—physical or financial jeopardy
  - ❖ Likeability—generosity
  - ❖ Admiration—skill, expertise, accomplishment
- Show how your hero is stuck or tolerating a negative situation

Step Two: The Crisis

Reveal the single event that forced your hero to begin taking action to solve her problem. Identify her specific goal, deliberation, and failures before choosing the approach you're promoting

- Reveal the tipping point for your hero
- Identify the specific, visible goal, or finish line
- Describe your hero's questions, fears, hesitations, and false starts

- Reveal how the hero heard about your product or process
- Tell us why she chose *your* approach

Step Three: Pursuit

Present the actual steps your hero took to accomplish the goal.

- Portray the moment your hero began using your process
- Take us through some of the specific actions and tasks

Step Four: Conflict

Describe the external and internal obstacles the hero faced on this journey.

- Reveal the problems and setbacks
- Portray negative people and internal fears
- Show how your principles or process helped the hero overcome the obstacles and continue moving forward to success
- Use your hero's fears and resistance to replicate the fears, misgivings, and suspicions of your potential clients

Step Five: The Climax

Allow your audience to experience your hero's success. This is the peak moment of your story—the one your readers and audiences have been rooting for.

- Show your hero crossing the finish line

- Let your hero celebrate the moment of victory

Step Six: The Aftermath

Paint a picture of the new life your hero is living as a result of achieving the goal. Provide a vivid description of the rewards your potential customers can experience, if they only follow in your hero's footsteps.

- Mirror the setup with a portrait of the hero's new everyday life

- Include those close to the hero who are sharing in the rewards of victory

- Be sure these new circumstances match the kind of life your potential client or customer longs for

APPENDIX II

Case Study Interview Questions

The Setup

- What was your life like before you first encountered the problem you faced, or before you decided to take action?

- Can you describe a typical day during that period?

- How did your situation affect your family, and those around you?

The Crisis

- When, exactly, did you decide to take action to address your challenge?

- What happened that moved you to take action at that moment?

- What was your specific goal in trying to solve your problem?

- Was there an event or an ability that would prove that you had overcome your problem and achieved that goal?

- What, if anything, did you do to solve your problem prior to working with us, using our product, or participating in our program?

- Why didn't those previous solutions work?

- How did you first hear about us, or about our approach?

- What finally made you decide to give our product or process a try?

Pursuit

- How did it feel the day you took that first step and began our program? (Were you excited? Skeptical? Reluctant? Afraid?)

- What surprised you about this process? Was anything about it different than what you expected?

- What elements of the program did you find most effective or beneficial for you?

- Did others support you on this journey? How?

- Was the change you experienced gradual, or did everything come together quickly, or at the end of the process?

Conflict

- What were the hardest things about starting, and sticking to, this new regimen?

- Did anyone try to discourage you from continuing, or unintentionally make the process harder?

- Did you ever feel defeated or depressed? Try to cheat on your commitment? Want to quit? Give up entirely before starting again?

- How did you overcome those tough times— how were you able to push through the obstacles and setbacks and keep pursuing your goal?

The Climax

- How did you finally know you had succeeded— that you had achieved what you set out to do?

- What was that exact moment like for you? For your loved ones?

The Aftermath

- What is your life like now, compared to what it was before you began our program?

- How has this change affected those around you—family or friends or co-workers?

- What would you suggest to anyone else dealing with the problem you faced?

APPENDIX III

Corporate Client Interview Questions

The Setup

- At the time you began working with us, what was your position with the company, and what were your responsibilities?

- What was your company's financial situation before you began taking any action?

- Were you aware of the challenges the company was facing, or did it seem like things were going along nicely?

The Crisis

- Did you or your company suffer any specific crisis or financial setback that forced you to take action?

- What effect on your business—and your personal life—did this crisis or setback have?

- How did the crisis you faced affect your employees and co-workers? Your family? Other companies you do business with?

- Did you try any other solutions to these issues before you came to us? What were they? Did they work? Why or why not?

- When did you first hear about the benefits of our program?

- How soon after you were introduced to us did you decide to hire us?

- Did you experience any concern or hesitation prior to committing to our program? What worried you or made you skeptical?

- What finally made you decide to give us a try?

- What specific goals did you hope to attain by working with us?

- How would you know when your company had achieved those goals?

Pursuit

- What were the most effective steps we asked you to take in achieving your company's objective?

- What surprised you about this process? Was

anything about the experience of the program different than you expected?

- Was the change your company experienced gradual, or did everything come together quickly?

Conflict

- What were the hardest things about beginning, and sticking to, the steps we recommended?

- What personal challenges arose for you, your co-workers, or your families as your company followed our recommendations?

- How were you able to overcome these obstacles?

The Climax

- When did your company finally meet its original goals?

- What was that moment like?

The Aftermath

- What is your organization like now, compared to what it was before you began our program?

- How has the company's success affected your employees?

- How has it changed your own life?

- What would you suggest to anyone else whose organization is pursuing similar goals or dealing with similar situations or problems?

ACKNOWLEDGMENTS

To be honest, writing a book doesn't really require much help. You just sit down, start typing, and there you go.

But *finishing* a book—staying inspired and committed, acquiring the knowledge that will give it value, choosing words that are involving and entertaining and helpful and inspiring (and grammatically correct), making the layout appealing, and the cover alluring, and the testimonials compelling, and then taking it into the world with enough power and promotion to reach all the people you hope to guide and transform with your message—*that* demands a great deal of help and support. Those who provided me with that support deserve more gratitude than I can adequately express. But I'll give it a try...

Let me begin by thanking Patricia Fripp, an extraordinary speaker and coach who has been a teacher, a mentor, a champion, and most of all an incredibly generous friend ever since I took my very first steps outside of Hollywood and into the worlds of public speaking and business. She has introduced me to countless brilliant and accomplished people she knew would help me, including half the people mentioned below.

Those include world champion speakers Darren LaCroix, Craig Valentine, Ed Tate, and Mark Brown. Sharing the stage with them is an honor and a thrill, and seeing their ability to tell stories so masterfully and powerfully has been both humbling and enlightening.

Thanks to Matt Bacak and Daegan Smith and Russell Brunson for bringing me into the world of Internet marketing, and giving me the opportunity to work with them, and to spread the gospel of storytelling even when I was mystified with concepts of funnels and traffic and split tests.

And to André Chaperon, a master storyteller in the Internet marketing arena, for his ongoing guidance, and his willingness to agree when I said, "We should do something together." Plus added thanks to André and his wife Anita. It was because of them that the foundation of this book was born.

As for the book itself, it truly would not exist had it not been for Henry DeVries, who has worn so many hats in its development that I should really mention him in four different paragraphs. He has been a supporter and mentor since we first met. He coached me through the process of turning what had been a series of blogs into a book. And as CEO of Indie Books International, he and his team continue to guide me through the journey of publication and promotion that begins once a book is complete. So thanks, Henry, for your wisdom, your humor, your mutual love of movies, and especially your friendship.

Included in the team at Indie Books International, a special thanks to Vikki DeVries for her meticulous copyediting (and for stopping me from using dashes and ellipses in every paragraph), to Joni McPherson for both her artistry and her patience with me in coming up with the cover and layout of the book, to Devin DeVries for managing the whole project, and to company Chairman (and Henry's sidekick) Mark LeBlanc for his help, generosity, and friendship, and for teaching me why a book should cost twenty bucks.

Deepest thanks as well to Stephen Woessner, whose wise counsel is invaluable, who has graciously opened so many doors for me through his Onward Nation podcast and his coaching, and who is simply a joy to talk to and work with.

Finally, huge but inadequate acknowledgment to my two biggest supporters...

Thanks to my assistant Nevada Grey, without whose tireless, devoted, and unmatchable help and guidance my business would grind to a halt—and without whose friendship my life would be far less fun and fulfilling.

And to my wife Vicki—always my biggest fan, always my most faithful promoter, and always my most appreciative audience—thanks for a lifetime of love and support...and great stories.

ABOUT THE AUTHOR

Michael Hauge helps people who want to make more money, and change more lives, by creating emotionally powerful stories.

He has been one of Hollywood's top script consultants, story experts and speakers since 1983, working with screenwriters, filmmakers, studios and fiction writers on their screenplays and novels. Today Michael coaches professional speakers, business leaders, marketers, consultants and attorneys, helping transform their stories, audiences and profits using the principles and methods of Hollywood's most successful movies.

Michael has consulted with every major Hollywood studio, and has worked on projects starring Will Smith, Julia Roberts, Tom Cruise, Reese Witherspoon and Morgan Freeman. He is regularly called on by Overbrook Entertainment, where he has consulted on the scripts for *I Am Legend*, *Hancock*, *The Karate Kid*, *Concussion*, *Suicide Squad* and *Bright*, among many others.

The best selling author of *Selling Your Story in*

60 *Seconds* and the 20th Anniversary Edition of his classic book *Writing Screenplays That Sell*, Michael has delighted and inspired more than 80,000 participants worldwide through his lectures and workshops on the art, craft and business of storytelling.

For information on his coaching services, speaking engagements and products, and for an abundance of information on all aspects of storytelling, visit his website at www.StoryMastery.com.